THE RAILWAYS OF
BLACKPOOL
AND THE FYLDE
VOLUME 2

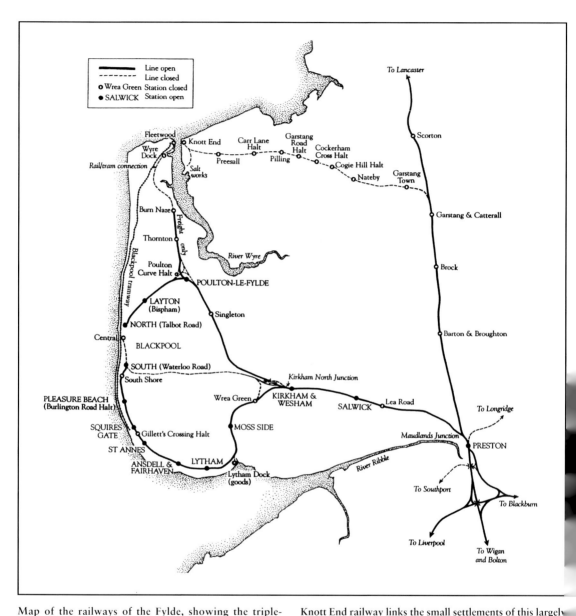

Map of the railways of the Fylde, showing the triple-pronged approach to Blackpool from Kirkham, which irreversibly shaped the coast's geography. The coastal line meanders to the south, the Marton Line heads directly to the heart of the town and the northern route does a virtual 90-degree turn at Poulton, whence the line to Fleetwood heads due north. Across the River Wyre, the Garstang & Knott End railway links the small settlements of this largely agricultural belt of land. Today the Marton and Knott End lines are gone, leaving just the two passenger approaches to Blackpool and the former Fleetwood line as a freight-only spur from Poulton to Burn Naze. There have been more than 40 stations in the Fylde in the past 150 years – today there are 12.

THE RAILWAYS OF BLACKPOOL AND THE FYLDE

VOLUME 2

Barry McLoughlin

·RAILWAY HERITAGE·

from

The NOSTALGIA Collection

To my grandchildren

First published in 2009

British Library Cataloguing in Publication Data

A catalogue record for this book is available from the British Library.

ISBN 978 1 85794 315 3

Silver Link Publishing Ltd
The Trundle
Ringstead Road
Great Addington
Kettering
Northants NN14 4BW

Tel/Fax: 01536 330588
email: sales@nostalgiacollection.com
Website: www.nostalgiacollection.com

Printed and bound in the Czech Republic

A Silver Link book
from
The NOSTALGIA *Collection*

ACKNOWLEDGEMENTS

The author would like to thank, among many others, Malcolm Richardson, Paul Nettleton, Ron Herbert, Jack Fenton, Shirley Peden, John Hillmer, Julie Humphrey, Tim Shuttleworth, John Goy, Glynn Hague, John Ryan, Philip Higgs, Blackpool & Fylde Rail Users' Association, and his family for their help and support in the production of this book. Where no source is given, pictures are from the author's collection. All fees for photographs by Frank Dean from the Malcolm Richardson collection have been donated to the Alzheimer's Society in memory of Jeffrey Richardson.

AUTHOR'S NOTE

The structure of this book broadly parallels that of Volume 1, with chapters covering the stations and lines geographically, then a sequence of thematic chapters. It is hoped that this will make cross-referring between the two volumes easier for the reader. All the material is new, however.

CONTENTS

A seagull's-eye view of Blackpool and its railways: this dramatic aerial panorama by Blackpool-based John Whittaker, a former British Aircraft Corporation (now British Aerospace) photographer, shows Central Station (bottom), with its 14 platforms, just eight months before its closure on 1 November 1964. John was one of the chief photographers at the company's Warton plant in Lancashire, and occasionally he took his camera 'aloft'. In February 1964 he found himself in an English Electric 'Canberra' flying over Blackpool ... and what a result!

In the top right is the resort's other main station, Blackpool North, which survives today, though only as the former excursion platforms. Central's own eight excursion platforms are immediately to the right of the main station. The small structure between the two, the toilet block, is the only surviving building apart from the railwaymen's hostel in Central Drive.

The picture underlines graphically just how better-placed was Central Station than North, which was located on the fringes of the town centre. The loss of the station at the foot of the Tower – a stone's throw from the famous Golden Mile – is still regarded by many as one of Blackpool's greatest planning mistakes. In Victorian times there were even plans to connect the two stations, but the density of development in the town centre – not least the massive Winter Gardens complex, almost midway between them – put paid to these proposals.

Blackpool's other surviving set of tracks, of course, belongs to the seafront tramway, now the subject of a multi-million-pound light rail redevelopment scheme. *John Whittaker*

INTRODUCTION: BLACKPOOL – IS THE TIDE TURNING?

A quarter of a mile from the wind-whipped Irish Sea coast, a solitary rail-built buffer stop symbolises the eclipse of the railway in Blackpool. It stands as an insentient sentinel at the end of the truncated single-track branch to unstaffed Blackpool South Station – a route that once whisked millions of expectant holidaymakers to the threshold of the Golden Mile.

The line used to run another 1¼ miles north to Blackpool Central Station, which, during the holiday season, was one of Britain's busiest termini outside London, with 14 platforms. Today the branch to Blackpool South is worked by an hourly 'Pacer' service, with main-line trains concentrated on Blackpool North nearer the town centre.

But in 2008 there were stirrings of a resurgence, with improvements on the Blackpool North line, the launch of a Community Rail Partnership on the coastal branch, regeneration of the seafront tramway and a genuine possibility of the line to Fleetwood being reinstated.

Like that buffer stop at South Station, Blackpool was built by the railway. It transformed a tiny coastal settlement, on a windswept peninsula, into the world's first mass working-class tourist resort in the 19th century.

The town of the Tower, Golden Mile and three piers has always had a reciprocal relationship with the railway since it reached the resort in 1846. The two have been mutually – and sometimes incestuously – interdependent. In the mid-19th century the railway was the impetus for a social and economic revolution as factory workers from the industrial North flocked to the seaside. In return, the phenomenal passenger figures into Blackpool between the 1850s and 1950s helped the railway operators – Preston & Wyre, L&Y/LNWR Joint, then LMS and finally BR – reap vast rewards in a largely monopolistic market.

In a single month in 1927, for example, the LMS carried more than 700,000 people to see the autumn Illuminations, and on one Saturday alone 105,000 people took the train to Blackpool. On Illuminations Saturdays up to 42 special trains could pass through Preston en route to the resort. During the 1937 'Lights', the LMS transported more than 600,000 passengers to Blackpool in 1,200 trains, from as far afield as the South West and Scotland. On the busiest single Saturday that season, 9 October, Blackpool Central and North Stations handled 107 specials on their 29 platforms. Nearly three million tickets were collected in the Blackpool area that year.

The scale of the traffic created major challenges for the signalling system: nine signal boxes stood between Maudland Viaduct in Preston and Kirkham North Junction inclusive, and five more between Kirkham and Blackpool South. To increase capacity, Intermediate Block Signalling was provided on both down lines at Ashton, Spen Lane and Bradkirk, and at Marton and Plumpton on the 'New Line' to Blackpool South and Central.

For several decades, however, that beautiful and symbiotic friendship between railway and resort has been inexorably breaking down, as the fortunes of the resort itself have begun to sink. Nowhere is this decline more evident than on the site of the former Central Station, at the foot of the Tower, which once funnelled millions of visitors on to the seafront every year. The site is still not properly redeveloped even though it was designated as the location of Blackpool's ill-fated supercasino plans. With a particular piquancy, much of the site is now occupied by that symbol of the rival form of transport that ultimately sealed Central's fate – a car park. Meanwhile, the former fast line from Central through Marton, which opened in 1903, is now the Yeadon Way link road to the M55.

By making it easier for tourists from far afield to get to and from Blackpool in a single day, the expansion of the road network at the expense of rail inflicted great damage on Blackpool's hotel trade, with the resort increasingly becoming a day-trip destination.

Only Blackpool North retains a sprawling eight-platform layout, and it is believed to have the biggest concentration of semaphore signals of any main-line terminus in the country. (And, incredibly, this was just the excursion platforms, the main station site having been converted into a superstore in the 1970s.)

The Chairman of the Blackpool & Fylde Rail Users' Association (BAFRUA), Paul Nettleton, says: 'Blackpool owes its very existence to the railway and it has foolishly turned its back on its heritage. It seems more than a coincidence that the town has been in decline since the mid-1960s, which was the same time Central closed.'

Virgin valedictory

It was in the early 1960s that the reciprocal relationship between resort and rail began to fragment, and the aftermath of that schism is

The eight platforms of the modern Blackpool North Station curve towards the array of semaphore signals with the Tower in the background in April 1996. 'Sprinters' wait in Platforms 6 and 8. The tracks to the original Talbot Road/Dickson Road terminus were to the left, near the

1939 multi-storey car park, one of the first of its kind in the country and used for aircraft component production during the Second World War. The station received a £700,000 facelift from Railtrack in the late 1990s. *Malcolm Richardson*

still evident in the town nearly half a century later. After the withdrawal of all Virgin's trains to the resort in 2003, as described in Volume 1, the operator dealt a final symbolic blow to its short-lived rail blueprint for the Fylde Coast when it removed the nameplates from *Blackpool Voyager*. Paul Nettleton called the removal of the plates 'the final insult', and Brian Grey, Chairman of the North West branch of the rail campaign group Railfuture, said: 'Liverpool and Blackpool now have no Virgin CrossCountry service, and it seems nobody can give a date when these vital connections will be restored.'

This has coincided with the decline of Blackpool tourism generally as holidaymakers seek sunnier climes abroad, and the resort becomes increasingly dependent on short-break tourists and stag-night revellers. Crowded trains into Blackpool North pass the miles of carriage sidings – largely empty now – that once housed the phalanxes of pre-Beeching spare excursion carriages for the holiday trade. At one time these carriages would have been enlisted to strengthen trains to meet peak demand, but now train fleets are at full stretch with no slack as the operators sweat their assets with a vengeance. (In the 1990s the carriage sidings were used to store sets of disused electric multiple units as well as some Class 120 and 121 DMUs, and more recently Class 142 'Pacers'. They are still used for carriage cleaning and other servicing jobs.)

A survey by the former Rail Passengers' Committee for the North West – the region's statutory watchdog, now succeeded by the national organisation Passenger Focus – found that the overcrowding was often due directly to train delays. The survey was carried out while former operator First North Western was still in charge.

In March 2008, asked if there were any plans to strengthen services to tackle peak overcrowding, Northern's Media Relations Manager Carolyn Watson told me: 'We work closely with local authorities and other parties across our network to discuss seasonal or event requirements and where possible we do strengthen services to meet demand – for example, Cumbrian Coast summer services. However … we have a finite resource and many demands.'

Electrification has been a long-dreamed-of aspiration for the Blackpool-Preston-Manchester route. Many schemes have been proposed but all appear to have failed to provide what in today's language would be called a 'business case'. Supporters of electrification, including BAFRUA, believe that Whitehall 'short-termism' is largely to blame for the failure to wire up the Fylde.

Former BR Operations Manager Peter Rayner, in the April 2008 issue of *Railwatch*, the magazine of Railfuture, said that Virgin's much-hyped advocacy of biofuels for rail must not be promoted as a way to avoid electrification. He wrote: 'The Government should be extending electrification – by authorising small, easy schemes like Fylde Coast electrification or connecting Manchester to Preston… Then we can go forward with main-line electrification, starting in five years' time with the Great Western and Midland Main Lines. That would be a strategic approach.'

THE RAILWAYS OF BLACKPOOL AND THE FYLDE

1.
CENTRAL SENTIMENT

The railway was a major employer in Blackpool, and Central Station was its hub. Former Blackpool Central railwayman Michael Carr, who appears in the first volume of this book, has dug into a fresh treasure-trove of memories of the famous terminus, particularly about the two old Barton Wright tank engines used as stationary boilers for heating carriages, also featured in Volume 1.

Mr Carr, a former Blackpool councillor, guard, porter and signaller, recalls:

'During the winter of 1961/62 I worked on firing them. We started at midnight, first lighting the fires with fire-lighters and spare wood, gradually building the firebox to its full capacity, which came around 3.30am when the steam was sent out to the six platforms and the slip road where the trains were stabled overnight for pre-heating

There were two of us on the night shift. The main duty was to heat the flagship train of that era, the 10.00am to Euston, once it was set in place. This proved very difficult and we had many visits from the station master as to why no steam was

going through all the way to No 2 platform. The boilers were fuelled by coke and, unlike the train engines with their Yorkshire coal, which burned through to ash, the coke tended to clinker very hard on the firebars. It was the main duty on the day shift to get them freed up for the night duty staff.

The wagons of coke had also to be emptied in readiness for the night; a few tons a day were shifted day and night. It must have been all this work that has kept my weight from what is was then to similar now!

We also had a key for the gate on the old gents' toilet block, which is still there, and on the New Bonny Street wall there is a plaque I paid for the Civic Trust to have made and put up with my name on it. The then Mayor, Councillor Maxine Callow, kindly came to unveil it.'

Near-contemporaries of Mr Carr included Wrea Green vicar the Rev Jack Wixon, a teenage recruit to the booking office, and former linesman and platelayer Jim Clancy of Layton. 'When we had to put in new rails and sleepers,' Mr Clancy told the *Blackpool Gazette*, 'we would do the job on night shift at Central Station back in steam days. It was hard work because we had to do it all by hand. Looking back, they were happy times and I worked with very nice men. I got to know a lot of the drivers and firemen on the steam trains, which were always kept clean and shiny. It was a shame they took steam away.'

Another renowned veteran Blackpool

Left Again, the remarkably convenient location of Blackpool Central Station is vividly illustrated in this aerial view of part of the Golden Mile. The Palace ballroom is to the left of the Tower and the Woolworth's building to the right, and the red-brick sprawl of suburban Blackpool spreads out into the distance. The Tower, 518ft 9in tall, opened in 1894 and its centenary celebrations in 1994 coincided with the 30th anniversary of the closure of the massive terminus, which was fronted by an elegant brick and terracotta façade. *Aero Pictorial Ltd*

Central railwayman is Fred Laycock, who lives in Wrea Green. During the war Fred was a 'passed cleaner' at Central shed – a cleaner who was qualified to work firing turns on locomotives. There was no automatic ash-cleaning plant at Central shed so locomotives had to be dealt with laboriously by hand. Fred remembers dropping the fires on locomotives and raking out hot ash with no protective eyewear – a dangerous and physically demanding job. The reward for all the effort, though, was when he was able to act as fireman on locomotives between Blackpool and Manchester Victoria.

During the war Home Guard units were set up to protect key installations such as railways and mines, often recruited from workers in those industries. Fred remembers two former camping coaches near the shed that were used as the HQ of a local Home Guard battalion. He joined the Home Guard as a very young man after initially serving with the Auxiliary Fire Service. The large Home Guard unit was part of the Liverpool-based King's Own Regiment and was under the command of Major Birch and Captain Denby. Fred, who was also an active member of the footplatemen's union Aslef, recalls shooting practice on the rifle range at Rossall. On the nearby tramway, there's still evidence of the location of the sidings where fleets of trams were parked after taking troops from Blackpool to the range.

He also recalls that Blackpool Central had a wheel drop on No 2 road of the shed – and that a former shedmaster was a certain William A. Stanier, later to become the hugely influential Chief Mechanical Engineer of the London, Midland & Scottish Railway!

This superb study of the great signalling gantry spanning the approaches to Blackpool Central station dates from around 1921. The 28 semaphore signals bestriding the station throat are depicted in an official photograph from the Lancashire & Yorkshire Railway's Horwich Locomotive Works. The signal on the left (west side) controls the down main line into the station (where there is a further gantry) and the other tracks beneath the gantry are (from left) the carriage siding, up main, down excursion (east) and up excursion (east). The main station is directly beneath the Tower while to the right of the signal box, with their own water column, are the excursion platforms. Just visible to the extreme right is Blackpool's ill-fated Great Wheel, demolished in 1928 partly because it revolved too slowly for excitement-hungry patrons. One of its carriages survives as a cafe in the Fylde. *National Railway Museum/SSPL*

Right The sheer width of the trackbed of the approach lines to Blackpool Central is graphically demonstrated in this shot of the girder bridge at Chapel Street in March 1974, near the location of the early-1920s signal gantry picture but looking in the opposite direction. The gasometer is to the left and the floodlights of Bloomfield Road football ground are visible in the distance. (The pylons later had to be reduced in size because of the threat posed by high winds.) This is now the main link road from the M55 and Yeadon Way into the town centre, known as Seaside Way. The picture was taken nearly ten years after the station's closure, but barely a scrap of work seems to have taken place on the promised redevelopment plan. *Don Rutter*

Below A Tower-top panorama of the Central Station site and approaches at the height of the holiday season in August 1982. As well as the hundreds of cars and coaches, it shows (from left) the railwaymen's hostel, the multi-storey car park, the old station toilets, the new police station and law courts and the Coral Island amusement complex, and beyond them (by the gas-holder) the rugby league ground (now a cinema), the tram and bus depot and works (right), the football ground and Bloomfield Road bridge, also now demolished. With a telling irony, the multi-storey car park was demolished in the autumn of 1998 after barely 30 years. This area was to have been the site of Blackpool's ill-fated supercasino. *Don Rutter*

Above In happier times former Lancashire & Yorkshire Railway 'Radial Tank' No 10759 hauls a stopping train of varied and antiquated rolling stock into Blackpool Central Station between the wars. The adaptable 2-4-2Ts, designed by Sir John Aspinall and built at the L&Y works at Horwich near Bolton, were mainstays of Blackpool and Fylde services from their launch in 1889. Many of these feisty little locomotives survived more than 50 years on the steep lines of the L&Y system and some lasted over 60 years. A total of 123 passed into BR hands in 1948. *J. A. Peden collection*

Below With its formidably broad boiler, former L&Y 'Dreadnought' 4-6-0 No 10430 heads an express on the approaches to Blackpool Central in LMS days. Although the Blackpool lines were a joint L&Y/LNWR operation, crews tended to have stronger loyalties to the 'Lanky'. *J. A. Peden collection*

THE RAILWAYS OF BLACKPOOL AND THE FYLDE

The last express worked by a former Lancashire & Yorkshire Railway 'Dreadnought' 4-6-0: No 50455 prepares to leave Blackpool Central with an 11-coach special to York on 1 July 1951. It was scrapped three months later. *Frank Dean/Malcolm Richardson collection*

Former LMS 2-6-4T No 42481 approaches Central Station past the landmark gas-holder with a works train from Euxton, near Chorley, on 15 March 1961. These '4MTs' were designed by LMS Chief Mechanical Engineer Charles Fairburn in 1945 as a development of the earlier Fowler and Stanier engines, with a shorter wheelbase and other minor modifications, and were to form the basis of the British Railways Standard 4MT 2-6-4Ts introduced from 1951. *Frank Dean/Author's collection*

Blackpool FC's Bloomfield Road stadium – then still hosting First Division football – forms the background as 'Black Five' 4-6-0 No 45101 passes Spen Dyke carriage sidings at the head of the 2.00pm Blackpool Central to Manchester Victoria service on Saturday 29 August 1964. *Ron Herbert*

CENTRAL SENTIMENT

A typically bustling scene at Blackpool Central during the annual Scottish Weekend on 28 September 1964. A six-car DMU forms the 1.40pm service to Bradford, and also pictured are 'Britannia' No 70023 *Venus*, Class 5 No 45385, Class 40 diesel No D234 *Accra* and another 'Brit', No 70006 *Robert Burns*. *Frank Dean/Malcolm Richardson collection*

THE RAILWAYS OF BLACKPOOL AND THE FYLDE

Top Rows of parked carriages are stabled in the packed sidings next to Blackpool Football Club's West Stand in September 1938. The locomotives in the foreground are (from left) the station pilots, Horwich-built L&Y 2P 2-4-2Ts Nos 10723 and 10833, and L&Y 3F 0-6-0ST No 11468. *Frank Dean/Malcolm Richardson collection*

Middle The expanse of the carriage sidings at Bloomfield Road is emphasised by this view across the tracks from Railway Terrace on 11 August 1962. BR 'Clan' Class 'Pacific' No 72004 *Clan Macdonald* is on the turntable after working a train from Glasgow Central, while ex-LMS Class 4 2-6-4T No 42461 hauls a rake of coaches as station pilot at Blackpool Central. *Frank Dean/Malcolm Richardson collection*

Bottom With Blackpool South Station on Waterloo Road bridge in the background, Class 5 4-6-0 No 44949 heads a train from Nottingham to Blackpool Central as Fowler 4MT 2-6-4T No 42379 backs out after working a service from Newcastle via Tebay on 12 August 1961. *Frank Dean/Malcolm Richardson collection*

Above A scene of devastation near Blackpool South Station as 8F 2-8-0 No 48203 works an engineers' train on 23 May 1965, nearly seven months after the closure of Blackpool Central. *Frank Dean/Malcolm Richardson collection*

Below Back on the footplate: the late Don Rutter, award-winning cameraman and Associate of the Royal Photographic Society, started work as a cleaner at Blackpool Central shed in 1954, serving as a 'passed fireman' there in the 1950s and early 1960s. He worked mainly on the Manchester and East Lancashire routes on 'Black Fives' and 'Jubilees' before moving on to English Electric Type 4s (later Class 40s) on the Crewe and London services. His atmospheric photographs of the final years of steam at Central Station and shed are featured in Volume 1 of this book.

Above Advertisements for LMS 'Popular Trips' and the Huddersfield Building Society dominate the concourse of an apparently deserted Blackpool Central Station. The main platforms are straight ahead, though the barriers are closed, and the excursion platforms are to the left. On the right of the picture are the news kiosk and the left luggage office, while on the left are advertisements for, among others, Virol and the local *Evening Gazette*, which consistently charted the rise and fall of the resort's great terminus. *J. A. Garnham/Author's collection*

Below This is the Blackpool Central site today. New Bonny Street cuts through the site of the platforms, with the glazed-roof toilet block still remaining in the background. The multi-storey building in the distance (centre right) is the former railwaymen's hostel, where engine crews stayed overnight. *John Hillmer*

2.
NORTHERN EXPANSION?

After the closure of Blackpool Central and the run-down of Blackpool South, the route between Blackpool North, Poulton-le-Fylde, Kirkham & Wesham and Preston became the main rail artery for the resort.

First TransPennine Express Managing Director Vernon Barker told me in March 2008:

'Since the route between Manchester Airport and Blackpool was incorporated into our network in June 2006, we have seen a steady improvement in performance and an increase in passenger numbers.

We are working with our industry partners to further improve the performance and reliability of the service, and discussing with the DfT how we can accommodate the increasing numbers of passengers using the services between Blackpool, Preston and Manchester.

The latest National Passenger Survey scores have shown passengers are generally satisfied with how FTPE is operating. The new "Pennine" Class 185s, which serve Blackpool, have also proven popular with passengers. Satisfaction scores for punctuality, upkeep of the train, cleanliness, comfort and personal security have all increased.'

BAFRUA Vice-Chairman Malcolm Richardson hopes that Blackpool North Station will retain its eight platforms and there will not be any further sales of railway land at the terminus. There's also scope for a bus interchange in the Apollo/Mecca site, he believes. The station features in Blackpool Council's 'masterplan' as part of a 'gateway' redevelopment of the surrounding area. However, campaigners are wary of any attempt to slim down the current expansive terminus.

Meanwhile, the first six automatic ticket gates on the Northern Rail network started operation at Blackpool North in early 2008 to combat congestion and fare-dodging. Northern Rail reported an 8 per cent increase in ticket revenue and reduced anti-social behaviour. BAFRUA Chairman Paul Nettleton said: 'It should have happened years ago, and at least revenue will be protected.'

In 2007 the association protested against Network Rail's decision to 'switch out' Blackpool North No 1 signal box, effectively taking it out of use, though stopping short of permanent closure. BAFRUA claimed that it would jeopardise plans by operators to service more trains in Blackpool as well as hitting steam and diesel specials. Local signallers were also said to be angry about the cost-cutting plan.

Blackpool North No 1, dating back to the mid-1960s, controlled the eastern approaches to the station, including entry to the extensive carriage sidings. After it was switched out, it left Blackpool North No 2 – opened in 1896 – as the town's only operational signal box.

Mr Nettleton said before the 'switch-out':

'No 2 is at full capacity and couldn't cope with handling movements at the easterly end of the sidings as well as the ones it handles on a daily basis at the west end. If the switching out goes ahead, it will lead to the ridiculous situation of units having to run into North Station, which will incur access charges, then reverse back into the sidings.'

Despite the protests, however, NR went ahead with the plan, saying: 'We are confident that Blackpool No 2 will be able to cope, as it has often served for days or long periods on its own. Steam trains and other special trains will also be unaffected as these services require advance warning and careful planning.'

But Mr Nettleton responded: 'There are still delays at Carleton box when there are conflicting movements coming out of North.'

In the summer of 2008 it was revealed that No 1 box was not to be demolished but retained as a 'ground frame' to be used on an 'as and when required' basis.

In the autumn 2007, however, there was less controversial news when Blackpool North Station Supervisor Julie McLeod won the prize for best station staff at the Railstaff Awards in Birmingham. Meanwhile, Northern Rail Station Manager Jane Lennaine joined Forces veterans at a moving ceremony at Blackpool North on Remembrance Sunday, 11 November 2007, to unveil a plaque honouring railway staff in the resort who died in wartime.

For three-quarters of a century the solid and handsome red-brick Blackpool North Station building dominated the junction of Dickson Road and Talbot Road. At 9.31am on 18 August 1971 a white-coated and gloved police officer on point duty supervises the traffic at the crossroads. Work is taking place on the roof of the station building, with its impressive cupola-topped clock tower, even though it would be demolished two years later. The arrow on the right points to the excursion platforms, Nos 7 to 16, reached via Queen Street. *Ray Ruffell, Silver Link Publishing collection*

Above The staff car park alongside No 1 Platform at Blackpool North Station on 23 May 1972. Even in those days the trackbed was strewn with litter. Under Blackpool Council's 'Talbot Gateway' pans, the station could be moved back to its original site with a tramway link once more up Talbot Road. *Ray Ruffell, Silver Link Publishing collection*

Below The deep end-screens of the 1898 main station at Blackpool North dominate the background in this view taken on the same day. They were perhaps a measure to protect passengers from the gales off the Irish Sea, though the prevailing winds in Blackpool are south-westerly and the 'country end' of the station faced north-east. The staff car park seen in the previous picture is full. *Ray Ruffell, Silver Link Publishing collection*

Above It's 10.37am on the same day and the morning rush is over at the ticket office at Blackpool North Station, next to the entrance to Platforms 3 and 4. *Ray Ruffell, Silver Link Publishing collection*

Below A forlorn-looking Blackpool North Station during its demolition in 1973 to make way for a Fine Fare food store and car park. *Don Rutter*

NORTHERN EXPANSION?

Left A 'foreign' visitor to Blackpool from across the Pennines: Thompson 'B1' 4-6-0 No 61295, of Ardsley motive power depot, stands on shed at Blackpool North in the early 1960s at the head of a line of locomotives. The former LNER engines were sometimes seen in Blackpool after hauling holiday trains from Yorkshire. *Paul Nettleton*

Below Works outings remained a regular source of revenue for the railway in Blackpool until well into the post-war period. Another interloper from across the Pennines, 'A1/1' 4-6-2 No 60113 *Great Northern*, stands at Blackpool North shed, alongside a couple of short-trousered enthusiasts, with a Northern Rubber Company special on 20 September 1952. *Frank Dean/ Malcolm Richardson collection*

Ex-LMS 'Jubilee' 4-6-0 No 45721 *Impregnable*, with a train from Liverpool Exchange, is framed by the twin water towers at the end of the main platforms as it approaches Blackpool North Station on 7 July 1965. *Frank Dean/Malcolm Richardson collection*

Above With the Tower in the background, Class 40 No 268 departs from Blackpool North with the 11-coach 10.53am for London Euston on Saturday 21 August 1971. *Ray Ruffell, Silver Link Publishing collection*

Below The sprawling signal gantry, now demolished, outside Blackpool North Station dominates this view as Class 50 No 409 and Class 40 No 320 shunt empty stock on 19 August 1971. *Ray Ruffell, Silver Link Publishing collection*

THE RAILWAYS OF BLACKPOOL AND THE FYLDE

Right The train shed at North Station forms the backdrop to Class 50 No 418, bearing reporting number 1A45, with the 10.58pm to London Euston on 19 August 1971. A solitary young platform-ender leans contentedly against the post on the right, spotting book in hand. *Ray Ruffell, Silver Link Publishing collection*

Right At the height of the summer season, Eastern Region Class 31 No 5811 approaches Blackpool North with an express from Sheffield on Saturday 21 August 1971. *Ray Ruffell, Silver Link Publishing collection*

Below In the days when trains could be lengthened to handle peak summer Saturday traffic, an eight-car DMU drifts towards Blackpool North Station forming the 9.45am service from Liverpool on the same day. *Ray Ruffell, Silver Link Publishing collection*

NORTHERN EXPANSION?

Above The future has arrived at Blackpool North. In the days when 'Pacer' diesel multiple units symbolised the brave new world of railways, Nos 142001 and 142003, in Greater Manchester livery, stand at Blackpool North on a staff familiarisation special on 7 September 1985. *Ray Ruffell, Silver Link Publishing collection*

Below ...and the old order. Headed by Motor Composite No E51830, a MetroTrain Class 110 diesel multiple unit prepares to leave Blackpool North with the 5.35pm service for Hull on 6 July 1986. *Ray Ruffell, Silver Link Publishing collection*

Above In the latter days of British Rail, for through services from Blackpool to London a diesel locomotive would haul the train to the electrified West Coast Main Line, where electric traction would take over. On 27 April 1984 Class 47/4 No 47434 waits at Blackpool North to take the 9.34am Euston train as far as Preston. *John Hillmer*

Below In the mid-1990s 'real trains' – locomotives hauling carriages, rather than diesel multiple units – were still frequent visitors to Blackpool on ordinary services. Regional Railways-liveried Class 31 No 31465 awaits departure from North Station in late 1994 with the 10.00am (Saturdays only) service to Manchester Victoria. *Paul Nettleton*

Left Blackpool North is the largest terminus still controlled exclusively by mechanical semaphore signals. Many local campaigners want to see the imposing No 2 signal box, the largest of the surviving L&Y cabins, protected by listed building status. The lever frame was shortened in 1973 when the station was concentrated on the former excursion platforms. This is part of the lever frame inside the box, surmounted by the station track diagram, in April 1996 – its centenary year. *Barry Shaw*

Below left The worksplate at Blackpool North No 2 signal box, which was built by the Lancashire & Yorkshire Railway at Horwich in 1896, is still in place at the foot of the lever frame. *Barry Shaw*

Above right Class 156 No 156464 coasts into Platform 6 at Blackpool North in Regional Railways North West livery in April 1996. *Barry Shaw*

Right You could still smell the paint on reliveried and refurbished Regional Railways North West Class 156 'Super Sprinter' No 156466 with its gleaming green-stripe motif when it passed Blackpool North No 2 signal box heading for Manchester Airport in 1996. A year later it would have to be repainted again, this time into privatised North Western Trains colours. To the left of this shot was the site of a proposed £3 million railway heritage centre, which was to have serviced steam excursions from all over the country, but the plan was abandoned because of funding problems. *Barry Shaw*

 is made the _twenty sixth_
day of _June_ One
thousand nine hundred and thirty four BETWEEN THE
LONDON MIDLAND AND SCOTTISH RAILWAY COMPANY (hereinafter
referred to as "the Company") by _Ernest John Hutchings Lemon_
one of their Vice-Presidents of the one part and THE MAYOR
ALDERMEN AND BURGESSES OF THE BOROUGH OF BLACKPOOL in the
County of Lancaster (hereinafter referred to as "the --
Corporation") of the other part WHEREAS the -- --
Corporation are the owners of a Highways Depot situate at
Bispham in the County of Lancaster in connection with which
certain siding accommodation has been laid in by the parties
hereto at the cost of the Corporation partly upon the land
of the Company and partly upon the land of the Corporation
AND WHEREAS it has been agreed to enter into this Agreement
with regard to such siding accommodation upon the terms and
conditions hereinafter appearing NOW IT IS HEREBY AGREED
between the parties hereto as follows :-—————————

1.　　THE Corporation shall repay to the Company on demand
the cost incurred by them in laying in partly on their own
land and partly on the land of the Corporation the Sidings
delineated and coloured red and pink hatched black on the
said plan Together with such appliances (including signalling apparatus) as in the opinion of the Company were --
necessary　(such sidings and appliances being hereinafter

The railway ran not just on coal and water but on vast quantities of paper. These documents are extracted from a fascinating 'paper trail' surrounding the simple installation of the sidings to the new Corporation Highways depot near Layton Station (then still called Bispham), the first stop out of Blackpool North. First there's the original agreement between the LMS and Blackpool Corporation of 26 June 1934 to install the sidings, which runs to 22 clauses (*left*).

Then the following year there's a letter to the Corporation from the office of LMS Chief Commercial Manager Ashton Davies about the siting of a weighbridge.

L.M.S. INTERNAL CORRESPONDENCE. G.

Our Reference. J.5025.   Your Reference.

TO   O. Glynne Roberts, Esq.,
EUSTON.

From CHIEF COMMERCIAL MANAGER'S OFFICE,
EUSTON.

(Centre No 1.).   (Centre No 1).

26th March, 1935.

To be returned to
CENTRAL RECORDS OFFICE
Secretary's Dept.
L. M. S. Rly. EUSTON

BISPHAM. Blackpool Corporation.
Private siding accommodation.

Under an agreement dated 26th June 1934, with the Mayor Aldermen and Burgesses of the Borough of Blackpool certain accommodation was laid down to serve their Highways Depot.

The Corporation did not find it convenient to instal the weighbridge machine in the position indicated on the plan and it has now been fixed on the outside road slightly nearer the Poulton end.

Will you please attach this letter to the agreement for the information of all concerned.

CENTRAL RECORDS OFFICE
L. M. S.

For ASHTON DAVIES

In any communication please quote the reference at the head of this letter and address

THE TOWN CLERK,
P.O. Box No. 11,
TOWN HALL,
BLACKPOOL,
LANCASHIRE.

Telephone BLACKPOOL 25212.

- copy -

Tuesday, 26th November 1963.

Dear Sir,

HC/SG.   HY/26/63.
Layton Highway Depot, Blackpool -
Abandonment of Sidings.

With reference to the correspondence which the Borough Surveyor has had with the District Goods Manager, Bolton, under reference A 4806/KS relative to the abandonment of the sidings at the Layton Highway Depot, the subject of an Agreement dated 26th June 1934 between the Corporation and British Railways Board (then the London Midland and Scottish Railway Company), I have received instructions from my Council to terminate such Agreement.

Under Clause 20 of the Agreement it is necessary for twelve months notice to be given and I shall be glad therefore if you will regard this letter as a formal notice terminating the Agreement with effect from 30th November 1964.

Mr. Shackleton, who is dealing with the matter from the Bolton office, is aware from correspondence which has passed between him and the Borough Surveyor that the use of the sidings ceased completely in March last, that the Corporation from that time no longer required any traffic into the Depot, that the Corporation were desirous of being released as early as possible from further liability under the Agreement and that the Corporation were anxious that the Board should not incur further expenditure from March last and which the Board was then contemplating.

In the above circumstances I should be glad to hear that notwithstanding the formal notice required under the Agreement and which I have given the Agreement may be regarded as terminated on 31st March 1964 and that action will be taken immediately thereafter by the Board pursuant to Clause 21 of the Agreement.

Yours faithfully,

(Sgd.)   R.O.F. HICKMAN,

Town Clerk.

The final correspondence (*left*) deals with the closure of the sidings in 1963. A letter from the Town Clerk, R. O. F. Hickman, dated 26 November, explains: '... the use of the sidings ceased completely in March last ... the Corporation from that time no longer required any traffic into the Depot [and was] desirous of being released as early as possible from any further liability under the Agreement...' The sidings had lasted less than 30 years. Similar correspondence exists between the North Western Gas Board and British Railways, about the closure and removal of the private sidings to the Princess Street gasworks in 1951. *All Ted Dabbs collection*

A rake of goods wagons stands next to Crossley's timber yard near Layton Station in May 1959. BR Standard 4MT 2-6-4T No 80093 approaches the station alongside a warning sign still headed 'Lancashire & Yorkshire/ London and North Western Joint Lines'. The siding to the right linked the line to Blackpool Corporation's Layton depot, the subject of the correspondence on the preceding pages. *Frank Dean/Malcolm Richardson collection*

Layton Station was destaffed in 1994 and the old station master's house subsequently sold at auction as a three-bedroom private home. The destination board of 'Sprinter' No 156481 still says 'Blackpool', even though it's an up train. *The Gazette*

In 2007/08 Northern Rail lengthened some of its two-car Class 158s to three cars to meet increased demand on the trans-Pennine route between Blackpool North, Leeds and York. Eight centre cars were moved from East Midlands Trains to form the new units, which were dedicated to the route. With Carleton Crossing signal box in the distance behind the train, unit No 158756, beneath lowering skies, heads towards Blackpool North on Easter Monday, 24 March 2008. In late 2008 Northern was due to introduce Class 180 'Adelante' trains on the Blackpool North-Manchester route to boost capacity. *Paul Nettleton*

3.
BEAUTIFUL SOUTH

A Community Rail Partnership (CRP) was launched for the South Fylde line through Lytham St Annes to Kirkham and Preston in May 2008 – the latest sign of the once-threatened branch's revival.

It was in the dark days of 1982 that local rail commuters formed a pressure group in a bid to persuade BR to retain the last two through services from Blackpool South to Manchester Victoria. They were unsuccessful – but the South Fylde Line Users' Association was born, now the Blackpool & Fylde Rail Users' Association (BAFRUA). It has waged a long campaign for a passing loop to double services to half-hourly and for a new station to serve the dormitory village of Wrea Green.

Northern runs an hourly all-stations service on the branch from Blackpool South to Colne in East Lancashire. Pivotal stations include Pleasure Beach, serving Europe's biggest theme park, Squires Gate, for Blackpool International Airport and Pontin's holiday centre, and Ansdell & Fairhaven, which caters for thousands of golf fans when the Open Championship is held at the Royal Lytham & St Annes course. Adoption schemes have seen Squires Gate and St Annes – the only staffed station on the line – spruced up, among others.

BAFRUA committee member Glynn Hague, one of the association's representatives on the CRP, said the partnership provided 'a great chance to improve things'. In early 2008 the association was particularly concerned about late-running trains being turned round at St Annes, leaving passengers at the three stations to the north high and dry. Mr Hague described this as 'an easy option', and BAFRUA

Chairman Paul Nettleton said: 'We consider that the operating authorities take the easy way out.'

To mark the launch of the CRP on 17 May 2008, a two-car Class 156 from East Lancashire took guests including rail chiefs, civic leaders, councillors and BAFRUA officers to a special meal at the Station Tavern pub restaurant built into the former Lytham Station building. There was music on board the train, and restored blue and white Lytham St Annes Corporation bus No 19 was on hand to take the VIPs on rides around the town. It was all part of a national Community Rail weekend organised in connection with the Association of Community Rail Partnerships (ACoRP). At the same time Rail Minister Tom Harris announced government grants to support small improvement projects on CRPs.

The South Fylde CRP wants to develop the branch 'as a showpiece regional railway with well-used trains, a high level of community involvement, attractive station facilities and good co-ordination with other forms of transport'.

Lancashire County Council has always been heavily pro-rail, and the Council's Richard Watts, Secretary of the South Fylde CRP, said: 'The partnership will be looking at ways in which it can develop the case for more frequent trains along the line, perhaps with the addition of a passing loop to allow them to pass on the single-line section.'

Looking back on BAFRUA's formation, Paul Nettleton said: 'The early days were the very darkest ones. And it seemed for a long time that the coastal route into Blackpool, which at one time had been the most popular one, was doomed to close. No matter what we tried, or how hard we tried, it appeared the line was totally unloved.'

In a remarkable transformation, however, passenger numbers on the route from Blackpool South to Colne in East Lancashire soared by 20 per cent over the four years to 2007.

Added Mr Nettleton: 'It does seem highly ironic that the association, when it was first formed, was told continually by the operating authorities that passenger usage was low. Nothing could be further from the truth. The fortunes of the line have turned full circle and, with the CRP, together with greatly increased passenger numbers, especially at Squires Gate Station, things are really on the up. I can see that we're on the verge of something big if the recent progress continues.'

BAFRUA has published a 'hit-list' of improvements it wants to see on the line. These include longer opening hours for St Annes Station booking office – which Northern did for a trial period in autumn 2007. 'The initial reaction that BAFRUA has had is quite positive,' said Mr Nettleton, 'and now Northern is having another go at opening the booking office for longer. We also want winter Sunday services, the timetable through to Blackpool South early in the morning sorting out, improved stopping patterns at Kirkham, and an earlier and later start on Sundays to connect with the "DalesRail" service.'

Northern is believed to be sympathetic to the idea of a passing loop, which Mr Nettleton said would be a boon when the Open golf returns to Lytham in 2012. Northern's Media Relations Manager, Carolyn Watson, said: 'The provision of a passing loop would provide increased line capacity, which would benefit services along the route.' Regarding the CRP, she added: 'One of our station managers is seconded to, and we work very closely with, Lancashire County Council, and the other CRPs in the area. This relationship has been very positive and productive and we're sure that will continue with the South Fylde CRP.'

The line even has its own 'Rail Ale Trail', a guide to good pubs within easy reach of the branch. The leaflet was backed by organisations including BAFRUA, CAMRA, Transport 2000 Trust, local councils and Northern, with distribution around Fylde Coast hotels, tourist information centres and local attractions.

Looking ahead in early 2008, Mr Nettleton's deputy, Malcolm Richardson, said: 'There's no reason why some trains from Blackpool South couldn't even go through to Manchester Victoria rather than just East Lancashire.'

He also believes there is more potential for using Blackpool South to serve the nearby Bloomfield Road football ground. However, any hopes of extending the line to the stadium were scuppered when Blackpool Council knocked down the century-old Bloomfield Road railway bridge in 2003. The Lancashire branch of Transport 2000, backed by BAFRUA, had warned that the demolition would remove any hope of restoring the line to the town centre. Instead of demolishing the bridge, said the protesters, the resort should seek to restore the railway and emulate the busy station serving Bolton Wanderers' Reebok Stadium. The bridge demolition was part of the £14.2 million first phase of the resort's 'masterplan' to regenerate run-down holiday areas.

Another potential new rail route could be opened up if the long-closed link between Skipton and Colne is restored. Services from Blackpool South to Colne could be extended to Skipton, although there could be timetabling difficulties with long single-track sections at each end.

BAFRUA was one of the first user groups in the country to set up its own website: www.bafrua.org.uk.

Right This 1911 Ordnance Survey map of Blackpool's South Shore shows the rather problematic proximity of the two stations at Waterloo Road and Lytham Road. The latter, also known as South Shore Station, opened in 1863 on the original Blackpool & Lytham Railway. In 1903 Waterloo Road (just to the north) was built to serve the New Line or Marton Line, which branches off to the right on the direct route to Kirkham. Thirteen years later it became a junction station with the addition of an island platform to serve the coast line, and the now-unnecessary original station closed and services were concentrated at Waterloo Road (from 1932 known as Blackpool South), though the carriage sidings at the former were retained.

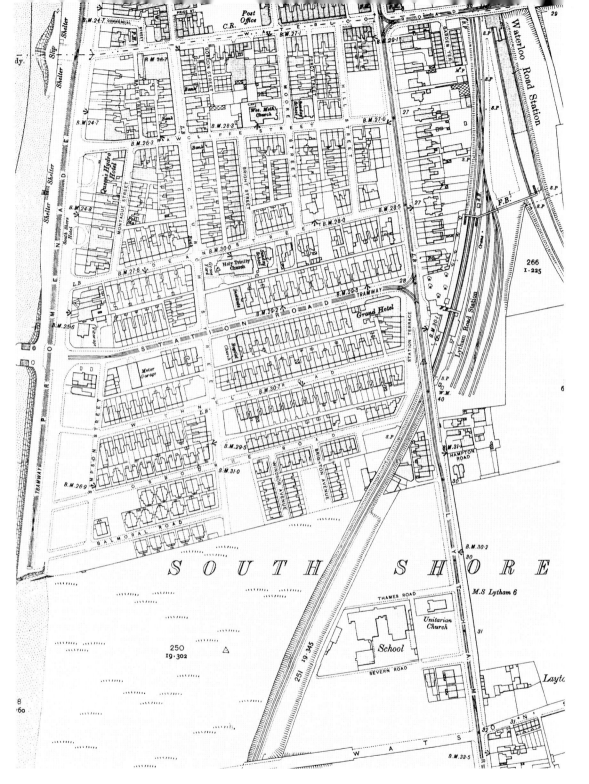

The coastal line runs south beneath the skew bridge on Lytham Road, across Watson's Lane (now Road) and past what is now the Pleasure Beach but was then, literally, a beach. The Blackpool tramway runs north to south along Lytham Road, and also branches west along Station Road to the Victoria (now South) Pier – though with the closure of the station the road, or at least its name, lost its raison d'être. The former South Shore Station site is now a car park for Blackpool Council's nearby Enterprise Centre. *Crown copyright*

BEAUTIFUL SOUTH

Above By the early 1970s Blackpool South Station was already showing incipient signs of neglect. Weeds sprout from Platforms 1 and 2 near the footbridge on 20 August 1971. Platform 1 is the only one still in use today, though the face of No 2 survives alongside the car park. *Ray Ruffell, Silver Link Publishing collection*

Below At 3.15pm on 20 August 1971, a two-car Kirkham-bound diesel multiple unit prepares for departure beneath the awning next to the ladies' waiting room on Platform 2 at Blackpool South Station. The closed Marton Line platforms, across the weed-strewn trackbed, have become an impromptu car park. *Ray Ruffell, Silver Link Publishing collection*

THE RAILWAYS OF BLACKPOOL AND THE FYLDE

Above Blackpool South became the terminus for London trains after Central Station closed in 1964, but in 1970 they were switched to North Station. A two-car Derby-built diesel multiple unit, comprising Driving Trailer Composite No M56251 and Motor Brake Second No M50968, stands at the station on 28 July 1973. Its destination will be just 8 miles away – Kirkham & Wesham. The road-level buildings in the background, which once housed a spectacular model railway layout, have long since been demolished. *Ray Ruffell, Silver Link Publishing collection*

Below Seeing double? No, it's not an optical illusion: replacement rail has been laid alongside the existing track during the £2 million renewal of the single-track South Fylde branch in early 1997. In the distance looms the giant Big One roller coaster at the Pleasure Beach, while a track machine stands near Harrowside bridge. Raleigh Avenue runs to the left and the lifting of the second track has allowed the new houses on the right to be built. The branch was one of the first lines in the region to be equipped with steel sleepers. *Malcolm Richardson*

Above The next stop along the line, Squires Gate, was a comparatively new station, opened by the LMS on 14 September 1931. This is a rare image of the station site in September 1925, six years before it opened. It was then known as Stonyhill Sidings, after the station that stood there briefly in the mid-19th century. In the distance, towards the now-demolished bridge and near the lower-quadrant signals, is the signal box, and to the right is the site of what would become Pontin's holiday camp; here it is literally a camp, a field of tents sandwiched between the railway line and the sand dunes. The sett-paved approach road to the left of the wagons remains largely in place today. The sidings were lifted and the 20-lever signal box was closed in March 1965. *Frank Dean/Malcolm Richardson collection*

Below After the demolition of its street-level building, the unstaffed Squires Gate Station began to look increasingly unkempt. However, this is what a little 'TLC' can achieve. The picture is taken from a very similar angle to the 1925 view. The Blackpool & Fylde Rail Users' Association has adopted the station, which serves Pontin's holiday centre (in the background) and Blackpool International Airport. The station is now in Northern Rail's corporate colours and an attractive waiting shelter has been erected, and access for disabled and elderly passengers provided. The association has also installed colourful flower tubs and does its best to keep the station clean and tidy. It is now pressing for the reopening of the passenger gate linking the station directly to Pontin's. The station sign now says: 'Squires Gate for Blackpool International Airport'. In the summer of 2007 passengers wait for the return working of the 'Sprinter' to take them to Preston – this train is heading for Blackpool South. *Paul Nettleton*

Above Gilletts Crossing, between Squires Gate and St Annes, was once the location of a small halt. On 25 May 1963 ex-LMS 'Jubilee' 4-6-0 No 45597 *Barbados* passes the site of the halt next to St Annes Old Links golf course in charge of a St Annes-Bingley return special. *Frank Dean/ Malcolm Richardson collection*

Below The ground-level halt at Gilletts Crossing (Old Links) was still open, albeit only for another 19 months, when the doyen of Fylde railway photographers, Frank Dean, recorded this scene in February 1938. LMS 'Jubilee' 4-6-0 No 5552 *Silver Jubilee* hauls the up 'Fylde Coast Express' during a rare seaside snowfall. *Frank Dean/ Malcolm Richardson collection*

Top Ex-LMS 'Patriot' 4-6-0 No 45514 *Holyhead* stands beneath the attractive but long-vanished awning at St Annes-on-the-Sea Station with the 10.00am Blackpool to London Euston train on 12 April 1958. Today St Annes is the only staffed station on the South Fylde line. The buildings on the up platform at which the 'Patriot' stands have been demolished but their large 'footprint' is still evident today, as are some of their rear walls. An interesting architectural detail is provided by the mock-Gothic arches set in the brickwork of the bridge carrying The Crescent over the railway next to the station. *Frank Dean/Malcolm Richardson collection*

Middle Diesel Prototype 2 (DP2) was a highly unusual locomotive built by English Electric at the Vulcan Foundry in 1961/62 using a 'Deltic' body and an EE 16CSVT engine developing 2,700hp. By the end of June DP2 was operating main-line passenger services on the Euston-Carlisle route, but by May 1963 was redeployed on Euston-Blackpool duties. Generally regarded as a success, particularly on electronics tests over Shap, it was the precursor of the Class 50s, but had to be scrapped in 1968 after being severely damaged in a collision at Thirsk. On 11 May 1963 DP2 stands at St Annes at the head of the 8.00am Blackpool Central to London train. *Frank Dean/ Malcolm Richardson collection*

Bottom In March 2004 First North Western started using locomotive-hauled trains on the South Fylde branch for the first time in more than 30 years. Class 31 diesels hauled the 06.40 service from St Annes to Greenbank (near Chester) and the 15.49 Chester to Blackpool North train, from Monday to Friday, for several months. The move, which attracted widespread interest from railway enthusiasts, followed the transfer of some rolling stock to the new TransPennine Express franchise, which left a shortage of diesel multiple units. On 26 March 2004 gleaming Fragonset-liveried No 31459 *Cerberus* waits at St Annes Station with the 06.40 to Greenbank. At the other end is No 31602 *Chimaera*. *Paul Nettleton*

The extent of St Annes Station and its goods yard can be seen (upper left) in this Ordnance Survey map from 1911. The railway line then runs through the ranks of new housing development, which it helped to create, towards Ansdell & Fairhaven,

passing the golf links of the Royal Lytham & St Annes Club. The Lytham St Annes tramway ran along Clifton Drive parallel with the railway until it was replaced by buses in December 1936; it closed completely the following year. *Crown copyright.*

ST. ANNE'S ON THE

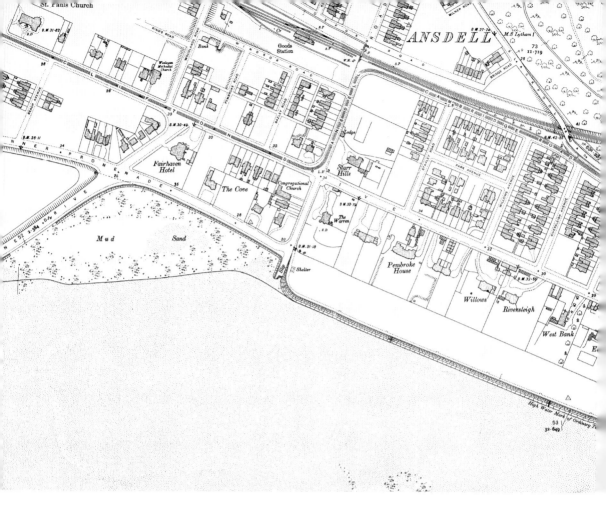

Above The stretch of track between the stations at Ansdell & Fairhaven and Lytham runs through a heavily wooded area, and it's difficult to countenance the fact that you're only a few miles from Europe's busiest holiday resort. This 1911 Ordnance Survey map, which continues eastward from the previous map, shows the L&Y/LNWR Joint line running from Ansdell & Fairhaven Station (top left), which had its own sizeable goods yard, through the woods – known today as Witch Wood – and past the cricket ground into Lytham. At Fairhaven the tramway turns sharply inland to run alongside the railway at Cambridge Road, then along Church Road into Lytham. *Crown copyright*

Left Former Lancashire & Yorkshire Railway Aspinall 2-4-2T No 10724 stands at Ansdell & Fairhaven Station on the coastal line to Blackpool Central circa 1928. *Edwin Ashworth/Ron Herbert collection*

Right On 16 June 1951 Stanier 'Jubilee' 4-6-0 No 45588 *Kashmir* outpaces a blue Lytham St Annes Corporation Leyland gearless double-decker bus, No 36, on a Crewe to Blackpool Central service, near the footbridge at Ansdell & Fairhaven Station. *Frank Dean/Malcolm Richardson collection*

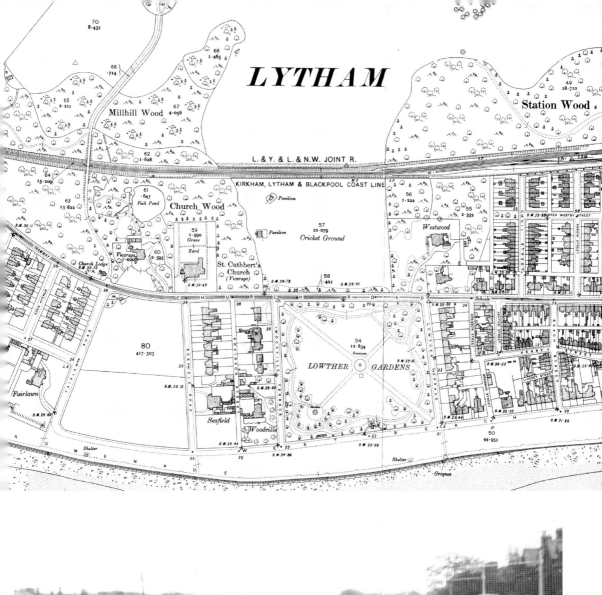

This busy scene in the goods yard at Ansdell & Fairhaven was recorded on 12 August 1965, shortly before the depot's closure. Ex-LMS 8F 2-8-0 No 48199 heads a local train of freight empties while the new order in the form of a BR four-car DMU passes with a Manchester to Blackpool South service. *Frank Dean/Malcolm Richardson collection*

Above Former LMS Stanier 'Black Five' 4-6-0 No 44732 is about to pass the signal box entering Lytham Station with a train from Blackpool Central to Manchester Victoria on 1 July 1964. *Frank Dean/Malcolm Richardson collection*

Below Every few years the suburban enclave of Ansdell & Fairhaven becomes the centre of world media attention as the giants of the golf world and Hollywood celebrities converge on the Royal Lytham & St Annes course for the Open Championship. The railway responds to the huge increase in demand by organising extra trains to Ansdell & Fairhaven Station, which lies right next to the famous course. A 'Pacer' waits at the station during the 1996 championship; the course is immediately to the right. *Paul Nettleton*

Above A special British Rail/Lancashire County Council headboard adorns the front of the diesel multiple unit that marked the reopening of Moss Side Station on 21 November 1983. The platform is on the former up line, and the down line to the left has been lifted, though the platform remains, much overgrown; the hospital that was one of the reasons for Moss Side Station's existence has been demolished. *Paul Nettleton*

Below The tranquillity of a village station is momentarily disturbed as 'Sprinter' No 150137 rumbles over the automatic level crossing and into Moss Side in the summer of 2003. The line is more usually operated by Class 142 'Pacers'. *Paul Nettleton*

Above In this rare view of a station that has been wiped from the map, with hardly any evidence remaining of its existence, unlike its neighbour Moss Side, ex-LNER Thompson 'B1' 4-6-0 No 61030 *Nyala* passes through Wrea Green with an impressive discharge of exhaust at the head of a train from Blackpool Central to Bradford in September 1960. The Blackpool & Fylde Rail Users' Association has long been pressing for the reopening of the station. Local resident and BAFRUA committee member Fred Laycock, a former Blackpool Central engineman, has been in the forefront of the campaign to reinstate the station to serve the village, an important 'dormitory' area for Preston and Blackpool. He believes the 1983 decision to reopen Moss Side instead was influenced by the fact that the platforms were still in place whereas those at Wrea Green had been removed. *Frank Dean/Malcolm Richardson collection*

Above right What a difference nearly half a century makes... This is the scarcely recognisable Wrea Green Station site today, from virtually the same angle as the 1960 picture, with the platforms and buildings obliterated. Class 150 No 150273 *Driver John Axon* rounds the curve past the site of the station on Bank Holiday Monday, 26 May 2008. The concrete post standing proud of the undergrowth on the far right is one of the few physical reminders of the station.

Interlude: The Marton Line

The climb out of Blackpool South on the embankment towards Watson Road bridge on the Marton Line, the direct route between Kirkham and Blackpool South/Central, was a demanding one, especially for a long train like this from a standing start. Ignored by the sole equine bystander, 'Black Five' 4-6-0 No 45078 heads the up morning empties on 21 July 1964 past what is now the site of the Palatine School playing fields in St Annes Road. *Frank Dean/Malcolm Richardson collection*

Another 'Black Five' 4-6-0 and its train are silhouetted against the sky, high above ground level, on the embankment carrying the Marton Line past Watson Road signal box – then known as Watson's Lane – towards Kirkham & Wesham. The line finally faded from the Fylde's railway scene in 1967. *Fred Nettleton*

Above A rare view of 8F 2-8-0 No 48491 standing near Vicarage Lane bridge on the Marton Line with the last demolition train of the day on 6 May 1968. *Frank Dean/Malcolm Richardson collection*

Below The Fylde is famously flat but this was one stretch of track where the railway passed through a relatively deep cutting, at the eastern end of the Marton Line. On Saturday 29 August 1964 a four-car DMU forms the 2.40pm Blackpool Central to Kirkham local service. *Ron Herbert*

Above Former LMS Stanier 'Black Five' No 44735 works the 1.45pm Accrington to Blackpool Central service (2P56) on the Marton Line on Saturday 29 August 1964, only two months before the famous station closed. *Ron Herbert*

Below Now you see it... The imposingly arched bridge at Plumpton was one of the few major engineering structures on the Fylde lines. Today it has been expunged from the landscape, filled in with spoil from the construction of the M55 in the 1970s. On 4 August 1956 ex-L&Y 'Crab' 2-6-0 No 42765 and former LMS Class 4 2-6-4T No 42403, running as light engines, prepare to pass under the structure en route to Preston on the Marton Line. *Frank Dean/Malcolm Richardson collection*

This magnificent image by legendary Fylde Coast railway photographer the late Frank Dean shows two Lancashire & Yorkshire Railway 3F 0-6-0s, Nos 12153 and 12175, with a Todmorden to Blackpool Central service, at Bradkirk in August 1932, having just diverged on to the Marton Line. On the right is the junction of the original Preston & Wyre Railway route from Kirkham to Lytham, which caused all sorts of operating difficulties because of the acute angle it created. Through coaches for Lytham continued to be attached to and uncoupled from trains on the main line to Fleetwood until 1874. That was when a new line was opened, which cut off the original junction and ran more directly and smoothly between Kirkham and Wrea Green. The original alignment remained in place from Bradkirk to Wrea Green for many years. In the early days of the P&W, from 1846 to 1853, the junction was also the site of a short-lived station, Lytham Junction. *Frank Dean/Malcolm Richardson collection*

4.
KIRKHAM CROSSROADS

Below Kirkham is in many ways a quintessential market town, but it is often forgotten that, with its neighbour Wesham, it was once an important area for textile production; cotton was processed in new mills that sprang up around the railway in the mid-19th century, such as Phoenix and Wesham Mills, though most of these have been demolished with the decline of the textile industry in Lancashire. However, Wesham is still a significant centre for biscuit manufacturing.

Bradkirk signal box was close to where the Marton Line diverged from the Kirkham to Blackpool North and Fleetwood route. Fitted with poppet valve gear, and with its distinctive high-stepped running plate and cylinders, Hughes/Fowler 'Crab' 2-6-0 No 13123 passes the box with a train from Blackpool North to Stoke in September 1929. *Frank Dean/ Malcolm Richardson collection*

Below The now-demolished 'flying junction' at Kirkham is seen here in August 1933. Coming off the Marton Line, ex-L&Y 3F 0-6-0 No 12323 negotiates the flyover above the Blackpool North route with a Blackpool Central to Royton service. *Frank Dean/Malcolm Richardson collection*

With its identity obscured by its reporting number, a Stanier 'Black Five' 4-6-0 heads an express from Blackpool past Kirkham North Junction in August 1966 while a DMU prepares to branch onto the South Fylde line to Blackpool South. Long goods trains were rare in the Fylde at this time so the lines of wagons parked behind the DMU may have been there for storage. *Jack Fenton*

In this broader view of the junction, at the height of the holiday season on Saturday 29 August 1964, Stanier Class 5 4-6-0 No 44749 passes Kirkham North Junction with the 2.20pm Blackpool North to Sheffield Midland train, due in the South Yorkshire city at 5.48pm. The line from the Kirkham flyover is next to the signal box, while the Blackpool South route branches off to the left. *Ron Herbert*

Running light engine, Fairburn 4MT 2-6-4T No 42295 and Standard 4MT 2-6-0 No 76081 pass Kirkham North Junction signal box on the same day. *Ron Herbert*

KIRKHAM CROSSROADS

Above 'Sprinters' to and from Blackpool North (left and right respectively) pass at Kirkham North Junction signal box, by now simply known as Kirkham. The fast lines on the right have been reballasted, and the branch to Lytham St Annes and Blackpool South diverges to the left. To the left of the signal box is a relay room. *Malcolm Richardson*

No. of trains passing Kirkham North Junction on Saturdays 12 0 midnight to 12 0 midnight During the summer season July 1st to Sep 30

Date	Year	Number	Date	Year	Number
Aug 16	1912	533	Oct 7	1933	588
" "	1913	578	Aug 11	1934	660
" 15	1914	336	Sept 29	1934	574
" 14	1915	331	Aug 17	1935	589
" 12	1916	374	Sept 28	1935	577
" 11	1917	335	July 18	1936	656
" 10	1918	296	Aug 8	1936	595
" 9	1919	382	July 24	1937	612
" 7	1920	425	Sept 25	----	606
" 6	1921	368	July 2	1938	578
" 12	1922	463	Sept 24	---	536
" 11	1923	488	July 8	195?	
" 9	1924	529			
" 1	1925	537			
July 31	1926	464	Aug 10		
30	1927	516	Aug 2		
Aug 18	1928	531	Aug 15		
17	1929	520	Aug 7		
2	1930	499	Aug 19		
8	1931	469	July 20		
July 30	1932	484	July 26		
Illuminations 6am Sat to...			July 24		
Oct 15	1932	596	July 23	1949	
Aug 12	1933	522	Oct 15		

Left This remarkable reminder of Blackpool's holiday heyday is located in Kirkham signal box, which celebrated its centenary in 1903. The board records the number of trains passing the box (when it was known as Kirkham North Junction) on Saturdays at the peak of the summer seasons between 1912 and 1949. The record total was on 18 July 1936, when the box handled a phenomenal 656 train movements in a single day. The box stood at the junction of the three routes into Blackpool – to Blackpool South and Central via Lytham St Annes, to Blackpool North and Fleetwood, and the Marton Line direct to Blackpool South and Central. Its 75 levers were split into two sections. Present-day signalman Steve Richards said that, at the time, the box was staffed with two signalmen and a booking lad – after handling 656 trains, he reckoned the latter must have had writer's cramp! One of the problems caused by the intense activity at the junction was congestion, leading to substantial delays. On the Saturday before the 1935 August Bank Holiday, for example, the net total delay was 3,653 minutes, or an average of 4 minutes for each train. *Paul Nettleton*

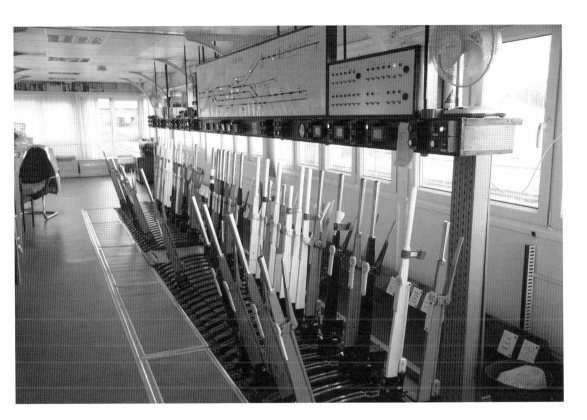

Above Inside Kirkham signal box on 12 July 2008 we see the impeccably painted and polished Lancashire & Yorkshire Railway lever frame, built at Horwich in 1903. Thirty-five of the original 105 levers are still in use at the box. It controls the section of main line between the boxes at Salwick and Poulton, in addition to the South Fylde branch. As well as being a Network Rail employee, amiable signalman Steve Richards is also a passionate enthusiast for railways in general and traditional signalling in particular. Steve, who once worked at the remote Blea Moor box on the Settle & Carlisle line and has spent almost his entire career on mechanical signalling, said: 'This job is a dying art. To me this is the proper way to do things. It's just about taking a pride in the job.' F. H. F. Simpson, who made an in-depth study of the Fylde's signalling with his son Nicholas, wrote in 1983 that the position of the levers 'involves much leg work. It is a box tradition that the floor be kept highly polished, as unsuspecting officials have discovered.' In the railways' heyday, the Fylde Coast boasted nearly 50 signal boxes; the Kirkham area alone had half a dozen, as many as in the whole of the Fylde today. *Paul Nettleton*

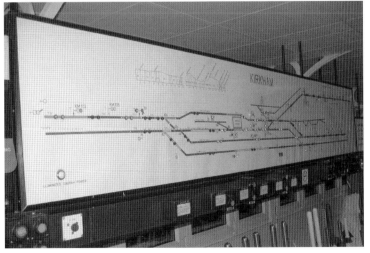

Above The track layout diagram at Kirkham signal box was photographed on 26 January 2008. Permanent way gangs were replacing the up and down slow lines during a Saturday night-time engineering possession and the tracks in the area were alive with activity. The diagram shows practically every track circuit illuminated – and note, too, the lever handles burnished lovingly by signalman Steve Richards. He also painted the levers and made a new 'Kirkham North Junction' nameboard for the box. Today, Kirkham still handles up to 180 train movements daily. *Paul Nettleton*

Above This quintessential goods yard scene at Kirkham & Wesham, near the North Junction, on 1 July 1950 shows former Lancashire & Yorkshire Railway 3F 0-6-0 No 52105 carrying out shunting duties in the sidings. *Frank Dean/Malcolm Richardson collection*

Below Industrial Wesham forms the backdrop as, between a tall lattice-post signal on the left and a water tower in the right foreground, Stanier 'Jubilee' No 45643 *Rodney* works 'Adex' 1X36 from Leeds City to Blackpool North past the sidings on Sunday 18 April 1965. *Ron Herbert*

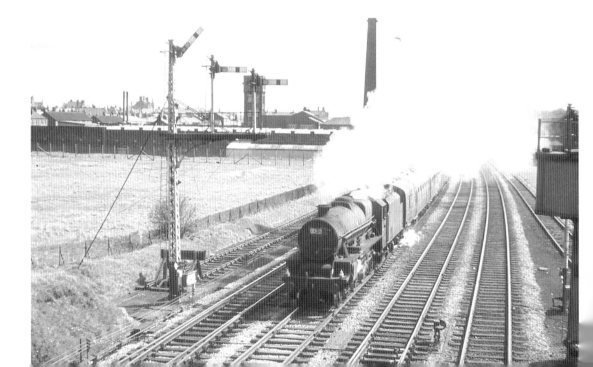

Above With its reporting number 2P63 scrawled unmistakeably on its smokebox door, Stanier Class 5 4-6-0 No 45202 hauls the 3.10pm Manchester Victoria to Blackpool Central train towards Kirkham North Junction on 29 August 1964. In the far left background is the former Wesham Park psychiatric hospital. *Ron Herbert*

Below Carrying the reporting number 1M89, a Sulzer-engined Type 2 Bo-Bo diesel-electric locomotive hauls a peak-season train of maroon coaches past the same spot at Kirkham & Wesham heading for Blackpool North in August 1966. *Jack Fenton*

Above In a wider view taken from the same place as the previous photograph, a three-car diesel multiple unit passes the distinctive chimney, since demolished, of what is now the Fox's Biscuits works at Kirkham in April 1972 en route to Blackpool. The Kirkham & Wesham station building is in the distance on the bridge, with the Railway Inn to the right. In the right foreground the signal gantry is now disused. In the distance behind the trees, soaring 150 feet skywards, is the exquisite octagonal spire of St Michael's Church; the church was rebuilt from 1822. *Jack Fenton*

Below The road-level booking office building at Kirkham & Wesham Station is seen in 1989. The station has repeatedly been the target of vandal attacks, and Network Rail staff were often called in to repair broken windows and kicked-in doors; there were even cases of fires being lit on the station. In the winter of 2007/08 NR demolished the former waiting room on the platform, which had been out of use for some time, and replaced it with a bus-shelter-style structure. The two remaining buildings on the platform were also expected to be demolished; used by permanent way workers, the staff transferred to new facilities near Kirkham signal box. BAFRUA Vice-Chairman Malcolm Richardson, whose own vehicle was vandalised on a visit to the station, called for the station to be staffed for longer hours in an attempt to deter the vandals; he said there was also a need for more safety investment at Kirkham, including the possibility of CCTV, to prevent passengers feeling intimidated, particularly at night. *The Gazette*

Above In May 1966 ex-LMS Stanier 'Black Five' 4-6-0 No 44909 passes Kirkham Station signal box (closed in 1975) on the fast lines, avoiding the platforms, at the head of a train from Accrington to Blackpool North (reporting number 1Z12).

Below The race to the west... Stanier Class 5 4-6-0 No 45005 (left) and Ivatt Class 4 2-6-0 No 43029 run parallel past Dowbridge, east of Kirkham, on 29 August 1959 with, respectively, trains from Shrewsbury to Blackpool North and Newcastle to Blackpool Central via Tebay. *Frank Dean/Malcolm Richardson collection*

Above At the water troughs on the quadruple-track stretch at Salwick between Preston and Kirkham in May 1929, thirsty 3F 0-6-0 No 12239 splashes past at the head of a service from Padiham to Blackpool Central. *Frank Dean/Malcolm Richardson collection*

Below Atomic Salwick: sheep outnumber people as a single-car Class 153, on a Blackpool South to Colne service, passes through Salwick Station on a cold, wet, windswept day in the spring of 2001. Salwick, east of Kirkham, is the least-served station in the Fylde. In 2008 the remote rural station saw just three trains in each direction on Mondays to Saturdays for workers at the nearby nuclear fuel plant. The plant formerly had its own internal railway system with a connection to the main line, and there are hopes that it could be reopened with the revival in rail freight and the acknowledged superiority of rail over road for transporting nuclear products. The Springfields plant has provided nuclear fuel fabrication services since the mid-1940s – in fact, it was the first plant in the world to produce fuel for a commercial power station. The site is today operated by Springfields Fuels Ltd, under the management of Westinghouse Electric UK Ltd. *Paul Nettleton*

5.
FLEETWOOD PHOENIX?

Almost 40 years after the passenger link to Fleetwood closed, campaigners have made extraordinary strides towards reopening the historic route.

The line from Poulton to the new town and port of Fleetwood was opened in 1840 – six years before the railway reached Blackpool. It was one of the first seaside tourist routes in the world, and survived the immediate aftermath of Beeching. Although passenger services ended in 1970, the 'branch' to Fleetwood was kept open for freight to the port's now-demolished power station, Fleetwood coal concentration depot (until 1983) and the ICI Hillhouse complex at Burn Naze near Thornton. Freight trains ran until the late 1990s, and the last traffic comprised tankers between ICI and Barry Docks in South Wales in 1999, after which the line was mothballed.

Now, however, the Poulton & Wyre Railway Society is planning to reopen the route, with the enticing prospect of it being fully integrated into the national network. The hope is that the line would act as a catalyst for social and economic regeneration of the towns along the former route, serving a proposed recycling plant and new housing.

Unlike some preservationist groups, the PWRS – which includes several key former and current railwaymen – has laid a realistic foundation for the reopening. It has won the backing of Network Rail, local councils and train operator Northern Rail, among other stakeholders. The aim is to reopen from Poulton as far as Burn Naze, then push on to Fleetwood as a major tourist attraction. Track is still in place as far as Jameson Road bridge, north of

Burn Naze. Rails would have to be relaid into Fleetwood and a new station built, possibly near the Freeport shopping complex at the docks.

July 2007 saw the society sign a three-year lease with NR for the former station at Thornton, where the platforms are still in place, and working parties have been busy cleaning up the site. Led by Alex Herschell, they have cleared vegetation and litter and excavated the base of the waiting room and old signal box. The lease covers the station and the line between the Victoria Road East/Station Road level crossing and Hillylaid Road crossing.

In 2007 NR also renewed the junction at Poulton where the Burn Naze branch connects with the main line, opening up the prospect of through trains to Preston and beyond. The year also saw completion of three positive feasibility studies. A final NR study was looking into the options for reopening and was to recommend which would be the best way to operate it. Options include a commuter/heritage railway, standard commuter railway or possibly even a continental-style tram-train route.

PWRS Chairman John Goy said:

'All parties are in agreement that the line should reopen; it's just merely a case of deciding how and who. Wyre Borough Council's Head of Economic Development has already stated that the opportunity for tourism based on a joint heritage/commuter scheme should not be underestimated, and we remain hopeful the line will go down this route.

We are also prepared to support NR and Northern should NR recommend that the line be reinstated as part of the national network. PWRS would work with NR to ensure all station buildings were reinstated in line with L&Y architecture and in keeping with the original route. We would also ensure that the line served the community as efficiently as possible.

Reinstating passenger services to Fleetwood is key to the social and economic growth of the towns along the route.'

He said of the lease from NR for Thornton Station:

'We have been given the green light (subject to planning permission) to start the rebuilding of the former ticket collector's office, ladies' waiting room, general waiting room and gentlemen's toilets. Our plan one day would be to have the society's offices run from here.'

The 170-strong society also plans to rebuild the former Wennington signal box, donated by NR in 2006. In May 2008 members witnessed the signing of a trust deed document by the first trustees, described as an important milestone. The formation of a trust provided a professional framework on which to build a successful railway, they said.

PWRS pioneer Eddie Fisher, himself a railwayman, said, 'Many groups have proposed the reopening of this line over the years but have fallen at the first hurdle. I firmly believe we have got where we are by sticking at it and not just accepting the first answer, which is usually "No".'

A study commissioned by Wyre Strategic Partnership predicted passenger numbers at a new Fleetwood Station could top 120,000 a year, with a similar number at Thornton and Burn Naze. These figures would depend on a through service between Fleetwood and Preston. Total costs were estimated at £12 to £15 million. The study predicted a possible opening date of 2012.

For more details, visit www.pwrs.org.

This 1908 postcard view of the station and steamboat pier at Fleetwood is looking across Euston Park in the foreground and the large, square area that had once been the Archery Ground. Berthed at the pier is a two-funnelled vessel ready to whisk passengers across the Irish Sea to Douglas and Belfast. They could step straight on to the ships via a covered walkway after arrival at the quayside station which opened in July 1883. Top right is Fleetwood's coat of arms and motto 'Onward', expressing similar sentiments to Blackpool's 'Progress'. *Commercial postcard*

Top Another shot of Fleetwood Station with the funnel of a steamship just visible at the pier. An advertising placard promotes the 'Electric Cars' from Blackpool – the seafront Blackpool & Fleetwood Tramroad, which opened in 1898, not long before this picture was taken. When opened in 1840, the railway was popular with passengers boarding ferries for sailings to destinations such as Bardsea in the Lake District and Roa Island (for Barrow). *John Ryan collection*

Middle People are thin on the ground in this view of Fleetwood Station from The Esplanade around 1911. On the right is the smart Queen's Terrace, designed by celebrated architect Decimus Burton, with its London-like neo-classical frontages. Fleetwood's halcyon years were probably the early 20th century, with 104,500 passengers sailing to Belfast in 1900. The service to Belfast was run by the railway company's own steamers. However, the opening of Heysham Harbour four years later hit the tourist trade hard, and the Fleetwood and Heysham services were amalgamated by the LMS on 30 April 1928, though regular summer sailings to Douglas continued until 1961.

Bottom The graceful semi-circular sweep of the North Euston Hotel is seen in the early 20th century. The hotel's name must be puzzling to modern-day visitors, who know little of its connection with the history of the LNWR main line from London. Sir Peter Hesketh Fleetwood's inspiration to found his eponymous new town had been a visit to the opening of the Liverpool & Manchester Railway in 1830. As High Sheriff of Lancashire, he served on a committee looking into the construction of a similar line to a port location on the Fylde Coast. By 1835 a site on the Wyre estuary had been chosen and the first stone was laid the following year. *Commercial postcard*

North Euston Hotel, Fleetwood.

Above A steamship could cover the 15 miles across Morecambe Bay from Fleetwood to Barrow-in-Furness much faster than the journey by train. The service was enthusiastically developed by the L&Y in partnership with the Furness Railway, which operated the steamers between the two ports, as demonstrated by this picture of one of the vessels used, the PS *Lady Margaret*. The crossing took only 1¼ hours and popular day excursions were organised from Blackpool to the Lake District, which was served by the Furness.

Below RMS *Lady of Mann*, seen in this 1938 postcard, was one of the stalwarts of the Irish Sea traffic between Fleetwood and the Manx capital, Douglas. Built in 1930 by Vickers Armstrong of Barrow, it served the Isle of Man Steam Packet Company for 41 years. The vessel's first season was spent entirely on the Fleetwood trip, carrying 185,838 fare-paying passengers. A study of who issued the tickets also shows how important the railways were to Steam Packet operations at that time: £1,628-worth of tickets had been issued by the LMS. Within a week of war breaking out on 3 September 1939 – only a year after this picture was taken – the ship was requisitioned and in 1940 brought 4,262 men out of Dunkirk during the evacuation of the French port, being damaged by shell-fire in the process. It later served as a troop ship and as a landing and headquarters vessel off Juno Beach during D-Day on 6 June 1944.

Above Handsome panelling and arches mark the entrance to Platforms 1 to 5 and the general and ladies' waiting rooms at Fleetwood Station not long before its closure in April 1966. Passengers on the last train from the station included retired driver Bob Etherington, who had worked on the railway since 1910 and had brought the first diesel train along the Preston & Wyre line. Platform 5 handled the Fleetwood boat trains. *J. A. Peden collection*

Below The ticket office at Fleetwood is seen beneath the ornate wrought-iron roof supports, with a British Railways van on the right. The station was known for its ornate flower displays and its ebullient stationmaster, Mr Oldham, who, clad in top hat and frock coat and always sporting a flower in his buttonhole, would, with his pet spaniel, wave off the boats across the Irish Sea. *J. A. Peden collection*

Above The main building of Fleetwood Station may have been a grand affair, but these are the bleak, rain-sodden platforms, looking towards the footbridge, water tower and signal box on the approach to the station in the late 1950s. *J. A. Peden collection*

Below Flourishing Fleetwood: a busy scene at the port's main station on 10 May 1953. From the left are LMS Class 2 2-6-2T No 41280 bound for Preston, LMS 'Jubilee' 4-6-0 No 45730 *Ocean* arriving from Manchester, and BR Class 5 4-6-0 No 73026 running into the station light engine. *Frank Dean/Malcolm Richardson collection*

Above With the cooling towers and chimney of the port's power station in the background, built on reclaimed marshland on the estuary, this is the distinctive quayside scene as two-car DMU Nos 50986 and 56269 approaches Fleetwood Station with a local train from Blackpool North on 7 September 1962. *Frank Dean/Malcolm Richardson collection*

Below LMS Stanier 'Black Five' 4-6-0 No 4948 rests at a smoke-stained Fleetwood motive power depot just after the Second World War. *Locofotos*

Top The Lancashire & Yorkshire Railway grain elevator on the rail-served docks at Fleetwood, pictured in Edwardian times, was one of the great landmarks of the port. Dating from 1882, the colossal building had a capacity of 30,000 tons. The LMS spared no expense in keeping the rail facilities for the fish dock at Fleetwood up to date. In the 1930s new electrically operated coaling appliances were installed, which enabled coal to be fed from railway trucks into the ship's bunkers four times as quickly as under the former crane-and-bucket system. *Commercial postcard*

Middle A former L&Y Aspinall outside-cylinder 0-6-0T shunter stands at Wyre Dock, Fleetwood, in an undated view probably from the 1920s. Research by Ron Herbert has confirmed that it is almost certainly No 11545, withdrawn in March 1936. The short wheelbase allowed it to negotiate the tight curves of the dock railway system. *Edwin Ashworth/Ron Herbert collection*

Bottom A line-up of locomotives at the former Fleetwood Locomotive Centre in 1990. Star of the show on the left, minus its tender, is ex-Great Western Collett 'Hall' 4-6-0 No 4979 *Wootton Hall. The Gazette*

Right This Ordnance Survey map from 1912 shows the extensive sidings from the Preston & Wyre main line to the Ammonia Soda Works (right), later United Alkali and then ICI, at Burn Naze, which opened in 1893. Burn Naze Halt is south of the works. The original alignment of the railway to Fleetwood continues due north across the salt marshes by the River Wyre, the stump of the old route remaining as 'Burn Naze Siding'. Meanwhile, the new alignment, opened in 1851, heads north-west towards Rossall, past the old salt works, which had predated the opening of the ammonia plant. It processed salt that was pumped as brine from the salt mines across the Wyre at Preesall. Immediately to the south was the huge Hillhouse complex, where ICI produced chemicals and which had its own power station. *Crown copyright*

Above Burn Naze Station, between Thornton and Fleetwood, was a fairly basic affair. A Lancashire & Yorkshire 2-4-2T is about to haul a local train over the crossing outside the station in the 1920s. Although the poster on the building to the right advertises 'LMS pleasure cruises', it is still headed 'L&Y and LNW Rys'. North of Burn Naze are few traces of the original alignment of the railway to Fleetwood, which ran somewhat precariously across 2 miles of narrow embankment and timber trestle bridge. Burn Naze was also the passenger station for workers at the nearby salt and chemical factories. *John Ryan collection*

Below The overgrown site of Burn Naze Station today. *PWRS*

Right The route of the railway from Poulton to Fleetwood, showing the mothballed line to Burn Naze. Track is down as far as Jameson Road. The line actually extends past the bridge but is currently inaccessible due to the bridge being filled in for structural reasons. The line beyond Jameson Road used to continue to the quayside station at Fleetwood, but the track was lifted after passenger services ended in 1970. It would be almost impossible to re-lay the line past Wyre Dock as much of the trackbed is built on. The Blackpool North-Preston main line is at the bottom of the map. The site of the former Poulton Curve Halt could be a candidate for a 'heritage' station. *PWRS*

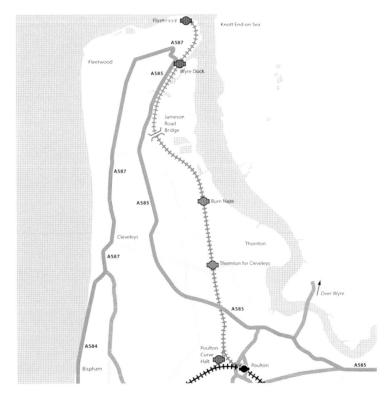

Below Work-worn Class 47/3 No 47370 hauls a train of tanks from the ICI Hillhouse plant at Burn Naze through the former Thornton Station en route to Barry. *Paul Nettleton*

Above The Poulton-Fleetwood line track is still in place at Hillylaid Road crossing in Thornton. *PWRS*

Below End of the line? A vegetation-encrusted buffer stop at ICI Thornton. *PWRS*

THE RAILWAYS OF BLACKPOOL AND THE FYLDE

Top and middle Before and after: Thornton Station in 1 June 2007, before the PWRS working parties moved in, and in November of that year, with work under way. *Both PWRS*

Bottom It might not be a train, but on 11 February 2008 the former Thornton Station saw its first rail-mounted vehicle for around a decade. This Komatsu 998 road-rail vehicle – belonging to Shovlin Plant Hire Ltd, which donated the hire cost, fuel and a driver – began a three-day operation to remove debris and vegetation on the stretch of line between the former station and Hillylaid crossing. Thornton Traders' Association also made a significant donation towards the cost of the low-loader that delivered the road-rail vehicle. British Transport Police closed Station Road crossing to allow the vehicle to be mounted and dismounted on the rails. Normally back-breaking work completed included the pulling of tree roots, platform scraping, removal of brambles and the cutting of the grass that had grown on either side of the running line. By the end of the operation, all 750 feet of the platforms had been cleared. *PWRS*

FLEETWOOD PHOENIX?

Up, up and away: this historic Victorian carriage was discovered by members of the Poulton & Wyre Railway Society being used a farm building. The extraordinary survivor is thought to be an original six-wheel First Class L&Y carriage that was in use when the old Preston & Wyre Railway was being jointly run by the L&Y and LNWR. When restored, it will eventually have pride of place as an exhibit on the revived route.

The painstaking operation to retrieve the carriage body, believed to date from the 1880s or 1890s, took weeks to plan. Fears that the delicate structure could collapse during the move happily proved unfounded.

The carriage body, minus its bogies, was discovered by chance on the farm, near the former Thornton Station, owned by the Hodgkinson family. Since the end of the First World War it had been home to a convalescing railway worker and a local midwife, and used as a chicken coop. In the past 20 years or so it had been used for storage, but despite its deteriorating condition the main oak frame appeared to be in good repair. Many of the original features remained, although over the years a number of internal modifications had been made including removal of a bulkhead to give a larger living space.

May 2008 saw the culmination of months of planning when the 3-tonne carriage was successfully extracted from the farm using a 30-tonne crane and flatbed lorry provided free by Thornton-based haulier and crane hire company Fox Brothers.

Sadly, elderly farmer Thomas Hodgkinson died before the carriage lift took place, but PWRS Chairman John Goy paid tribute to him and his widow, Eunice, and her family for donating the vehicle. He also thanked Fox Brothers for providing the heavy plant equipment to carry out the operation, and NPL Estates for allowing the society to store the coach at its secure business park.

Secretary Dennis Goy said: 'We would love to restore it to its former glory and see it carrying passengers. However, before we can start, we need to understand what work needs to be done and how much it will cost. The main thing is that we have saved the carriage from certain demise.'

The PWRS also had its eye on a former Leyland Motors 0-4-0 diesel shunter, which its owner, Lancashire Enterprises, had agreed to donate to the society.

Left The delicate operation to lift the carriage from its tree-shrouded site begins. *PWRS*

Above Nearly there: the Fox Brothers crane lifts the carriage body from the lorry and lowers it on to its new site. *PWRS*

Left Sign of the times: 'Passengers are earnestly requested not to spit in the carriages.' *PWRS*

Below Window seat: inside the former L&Y carriage. *PWRS*

Above At the turn of the 21st century, Railtrack spent £375,000 refurbishing Poulton-le-Fylde Station, including revamping the waiting rooms, reglazing the ornate canopy roof and restoring its distinctive platform clocks. Under the banner of Poulton Station Partnership, colourful floral displays have also helped revitalise the station, with blooms donated by The Plant Place of Thornton and hanging-baskets sponsored by local businesses and provided by Blackpool company Glasdon. Class 101 DMU No 101659 waits beneath the attractively repainted canopy with a service for Blackpool North in the summer of 2000. *Paul Nettleton*

Below The Open Championship returned to Royal Lytham & St Annes in 2001 and First North Western operated a special timetable on the South Fylde branch to cope with the demand from golf fans wanting to see the likes of Tiger Woods, Ian Woosnam and David Duval. In addition, the luxury 'Northern Belle' train also visited Blackpool North, taking passengers to the tournament. On 20 July, hauled by 'Royal' Class 47 No 47799 *Prince Henry*, the train is passing slowly through Poulton-le-Fylde on the return leg to Edinburgh after servicing and cleaning at Blackpool North carriage sidings. *Paul Nettleton*

Above A Blackpool-bound express passes an Aspinall 2-4-2 tank locomotive at Poulton No 2 signal box around the turn of the last century. The Fleetwood and Blackpool lines diverge at the other end of the station, behind the camera. *John Ryan collection*

Below Trains between Fleetwood and Blackpool North had to negotiate the curve between the two lines at Poulton-le-Fylde. Former Lancashire & Yorkshire Railway 2P 2-4-2T No 10802 arrives at Poulton Curve Halt in September 1946, with a local train from Fleetwood to Blackpool North. The Fleetwood-Preston line can be seen in the background. *Frank Dean/Malcolm Richardson collection*

Interlude: On Singleton Bank

The intensity of services to and from Blackpool is underscored by this sequence of photographs taken on the same day, Monday 19 April 1965, on Singleton Bank between Poulton and Kirkham. It may well have been Easter Monday.

The pictures are by celebrated photographer Ron Herbert, a 50-year career railwayman and former senior BR controller who lives in Preston. They were taken less than four years after the tragedy when seven people were killed in a collision between a DMU and a stationary ballast train on the bank (see Volume 1).

Left British Railways Standard 'Britannia' Class 'Pacific' No 70015 *Apollo* heads a Blackpool North to Coventry train – reporting number 1Z66.

Below left With a fine display of exhaust, Fairburn 4MT 2-6-4T No 42296 hauls 1Z09, a local service from Blackpool North to Preston.

Above Stanier 'Jubilee' 4-6-0s were among the mainstays of motive power for holiday expresses to Blackpool. The spring sunshine glints off the boiler side of 'Jubilee' No 45562 *Alberta* with 1X41 from Blackpool North to Leeds City.

Below With a rake of maroon coaches, and in smart green livery with white stripes and yellow warning panels, Brush Type 2 (later Class 31) No D5848 hauls an excursion from Blackpool North to Chesterfield with reporting number 1X06. The Saxby & Farmer signal box at Singleton can be seen on the embankment in the background.

And finally, much earlier – probably in the 1920s – a classic shot of a double-headed goods train, possibly from Wyre Dock, in a very similar location near Singleton. It is being hauled by two former L&Y engines, both designed by Sir John Aspinall; a '27' Class 3F 0-6-0 (leading) and a heavy freight 0-8-0. *Edwin Ashworth/Ron Herbert collection*

THE RAILWAYS OF BLACKPOOL AND THE FYLDE

6.
THE GARSTANG & KNOTT END RAILWAY

The 7-mile line between Garstang and Pilling had been opened with little ceremony on 14 December 1870 (though trains had been running for nine days by then). The initial service was an impressive nine trains each way daily, except Sundays, from Garstang & Catterall to Garstang Town; three a day continued to Pilling. All the trains were, like this one, mixed passenger and goods. Platform staff look on GKER 0-6-0T *Knott End*, built by Manning Wardle of Leeds in 1908 as Works No 1732, stands at Pilling Station with a train including some of the original coaches. *J. A. Peden collection*

Introduced in 1897, GKER Hudswell Clarke saddle tank *Jubilee Queen* hauls a short train comprising two antiquated carriages and a van. The line's first locomotive was 0-4-2T *Hebe*, which was hired together with four carriages, 24 wagons and two brake vans for the official opening. They were hired rather than bought after the construction costs outstripped their £60,000 estimated budget by some £90,000. *Hebe* was worked so hard that it had to be withdrawn for overhaul in March 1872 and was then repossessed when rent arrears built up. After the railway went into receivership in 1874, two tank engines were hired, services were resumed, stations refurbished and the debts eventually paid off. *J. A. Peden collection*

The eccentric but engaging Garstang & Knott End Railway ran from Garstang & Catterall Station on the West Coast Main Line (just off this 1959 Ordnance Survey map to the right), through Garstang Town Station and then across the Lancaster Canal west to Pilling, through the sparsely populated countryside and calling at Nateby, Cogie Hill and Cockerham Cross. The line west of Pilling had closed in 1950. *Crown copyright*

　　　THE RAILWAYS OF BLACKPOOL AND THE FYLDE

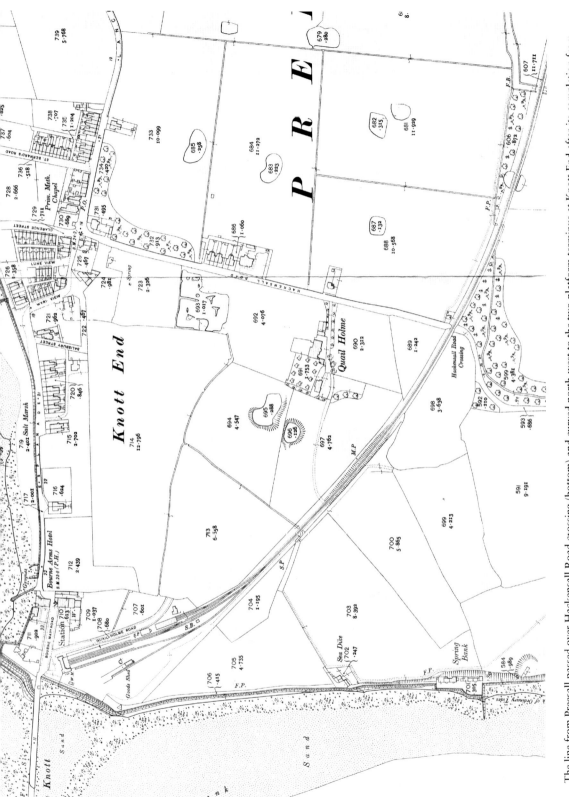

The line from Preesall passed over Hackensall Road crossing (bottom) and curved north-west to the two-platform terminus at Knott End after its completion from Pilling in 1908. The small goods depot is to the left of the station. A ferry still links Knott End to Fleetwood across the Wyre estuary. *Crown copyright*

Above The hefty 2-6-0T *Blackpool* was the biggest engine in use on the Garstang & Knott End Railway, and its wheel arrangement was rare for a tank locomotive. Built by Manning Wardle in 1908, and introduced for the salt trade the following year, it was one of the heaviest engines on Britain's light railways. *F. W. Shuttleworth collection*

Below With the development of salt mines at Preesall in the early 1900s, the ailing line received a major boost. In 1912 a short branch was built to the mines, and the trade in salt and coal totalled almost 80,000 tones in 1922. The line ran to this jetty on the River Wyre, from which the rock salt was ferried across to the salt works at Burn Naze, and a pipeline for the brine was laid beneath the Wyre. On the passenger side, meanwhile, the LMS increased traffic on the line to six trains each way on weekdays. However, a dispute with the United Alkali Company over haulage rates resulted in the loss of this vital revenue, hitting the line's viability, and passenger services were scrapped in 1930. The last train was worked by an ex-LNWR steam railmotor. *The Gazette*

Above Children and a cyclist are among passengers waiting at Preesall soon after the station's opening in 1908. Some of the crossing-keepers' houses along the route are still in use as private homes, though few other remnants of the line remain. In 2000, however, a Hudswell Clarke industrial 0-6-0ST was craned into position and 'plinthed' as a reminder of the 'Pilling Pig' at Fold House Caravan Park in Pilling. The locomotive is actually a former National Coal Board engine, dating only as far back as the 1950s, from Mountain Ash Colliery in South Wales. *Frank Dean/ Malcolm Richardson collection*

Below Seen from Preesall Hill through the leaf-shorn branches of wintry trees, the picturesque Preesall Station closed with the end of the passenger service on the line in March 1930, but the old building survives in this later view. *The Gazette*

Above Seven months after its complete closure, vegetation is already re-establishing itself on the platforms and tracks of Knott End Station in June 1951, although the station had closed to passengers more than 20 years earlier. *C. A. Appleton/J. A. Peden collection*

Below With 'The Last "Pilling Pig"' chalked on its tender, Stanier 'Black Five' 4-6-0 No 45039 prepares to leave the yard at Garstang & Catterall Station for Garstang Town yard with the final train on the former Garstang & Knott End Railway on Friday 13 August 1965. It officially closed the following Monday. The train was the daily freight from Preston (Ribble Sidings) to Garstang Town. The line between Pilling and Garstang Town had closed two years earlier. *Frank Dean/Malcolm Richardson collection*

THE GARSTANG & KNOTT END RAILWAY

7.
STEAM RENAISSANCE

Below Since 1998, when steam reappeared in Blackpool for the first time in 30 years, the resort has enjoyed visits from locomotives of all of the former 'Big Four' railway companies. It's ironic that the town has seen an array of locomotives that, during the original days of steam, would never have appeared in the LMS-dominated resort. One such was rebuilt Bulleid 'Merchant Navy' Class 'Pacific' No 35005 *Canadian Pacific*, which in steam days would have been confined largely to the Southern Region. The elegant BR blue-liveried locomotive stands at Blackpool North with the 'Blackpool Belle' in October 1999. The popular and energetic former Blackpool North Station Manager Barry Cole also set up a successful steam and diesel railtour operation, Lancashire Railtours. *Barry Shaw*

Below The 'Blackpool Belle' returned to the resort on 26 May 2001, but this time hauled by former LNER 'A2' Class 'Pacific' No 60532 *Blue Peter*, seen drifting through Poulton-le-Fylde Station. The locomotive, hauling a charter from Tamworth, was working a series of excursions before its main-line operating certificate expired. *Paul Nettleton*

Right There was another ex-LNER visitor on a rainy 5 November 2005 when Class 'B1' 4-6-0 No 61264 hauled an Illuminations special from Lincoln to Blackpool North, via the Copy Pit route over the Pennines. As with the other railtours to Blackpool, the hundreds of passengers gave a big late-season boost to the Blackpool economy. The impeccably polished locomotive is seen during servicing at Blackpool North carriage sidings. *Paul Nettleton*

Below By contrast, this is the type of engine that Blackpool saw regularly in the BR steam era. Former LMS 'Black Five' 4-6-0 No 45157 powers through Layton Station on 22 July 2000 with steam to spare, hauling 'The Fishwick Fellsman'. When this picture was taken, the Stanier-designed locomotive had clocked up some 10,000 miles in just two years of main-line running. As with many steam destinations, following the phasing out of turntables, turning locomotives can pose big problems. In Blackpool the stock has to be shunted into the carriage sidings, then the engine has to run to the triangle at Preston more than 20 miles away. If Poulton Curve was reinstated as part of the Fleetwood reopening plan, it would mean a round trip of barely 10 miles to turn a steam locomotive compared with more than 40 at present. *Paul Nettleton*

Above Although the West Coast Main Line skirts the eastern fringe of the Fylde, former LMS Stanier 'Duchess' 4-6-2s – which worked the top expresses on the London Euston-Glasgow route – only very rarely visited Blackpool, if at all. In the preservation era, however, No 6233 *Duchess of Sutherland* – one of the giants of steam traction – has become something of a Blackpool favourite, making half a dozen appearances in as many years. Just after 11.00am on Saturday 10 May 2008, with 500 passengers on board, the locomotive passes Fox's Biscuits at Wesham with PMR Tours' 'Fylde Coast Express' bound for Blackpool North from Sheffield. Kirkham & Wesham Station is in the background. *Paul Nettleton*

Below This is one of the most unusual steam locomotives to have visited Blackpool. In the steam era, Great Western engines, with their distinctive green livery and copper-capped chimneys, operated mainly on the Western Region, and the furthest north they would have reached would have been Birkenhead on services from London Paddington. On 17 July 2004, however, former GWR Collett 'Hall' 4-6-0 No 4936 *Kinlet Hall* arrived in Blackpool North on an excursion from the West Midlands. The smartly turned-out train is pictured coasting into Blackpool North 15 minutes early. *Paul Nettleton*

THE RAILWAYS OF BLACKPOOL AND THE FYLDE

Above In 2005 Blackpool proved to be a popular destination for steam excursions, with a 'Black Five' hauling a series of three steam specials from the East Lancashire Railway during the Illuminations in October. However, this is the engine that had started the ball rolling on Bank Holiday Monday, 29 August, when freshly overhauled ex-LMS 'Jubilee' Class 4-6-0 No 5690 *Leander* glided into the resort with a well-loaded Vintage Trains excursion. It is seen making a spectacular departure from North Station on the return to Nuneaton. *Paul Nettleton*

Right It's not just steam specials that have brought fresh variety to Blackpool's train services; diesels too have made their mark. This specially extended 'Sprinter' set, headed by No 156490, brought fans of Castleford Tigers Rugby League Club to the resort for their Northern Rail Cup Final clash with Hull Kingston Rovers on 17 July 2005 at Bloomfield Road football ground. And in the 11-a-side code, a highly unusual Class 31 and 33 combination – Nos 33108 and 31602 *Chimaera* – took Blackpool FC supporters to their LDV Vans Trophy Final triumph at Cardiff's Millennium Stadium on 24 March 2002. *Paul Nettleton*

STEAM RENAISSANCE

Left In 1961 affluent American Rogers Whitaker flew 3,500 miles from the United States to travel behind the world steam speed record-holder, ex-LNER Gresley 'A4' Class 'Pacific' No 60022 *Mallard*. Mr Whitaker brings a transatlantic greeting as he stands beside the locomotive's nameplate during a visit by the renowned locomotive to Blackpool North in 1961. *The Gazette*

Below And finally … an earlier 'Blackpool Belle'. Crowds throng the platform at Blackpool North Station to see the legendary 'A3' 4-6-2 No 60103 *Flying Scotsman*, possibly the world's most celebrated locomotive, when it hauled the 'Belle' to the resort on 8 October 1966. Note how smartly turned-out everyone is: suits and ties seem to be de rigueur for the men, as small boys clamber into the cab. After a somewhat chequered career, the 1923-built engine, now carrying its LNER number 4472, is a prized part of the National Collection at York, where it is being overhauled. *The Gazette*

8.
ENGINEERING THE FUTURE

As explained in Volume 1, infrastructure has been the big area in which the Fylde Coast's rail system has made gains under privatisation. Both the ill-omened Railtrack and its successor Network Rail have invested heavily in stations and track in the Fylde, particularly the latter during engineering possessions on winter weekends.

In 2005 NR carried out major track renewal work between Blackpool North and Preston, costing around £1.5 million, replacing old jointed rail with the continuously welded variety to make for a smoother ride.

One of the biggest and most important infrastructure schemes took place in early 2007 when NR renewed the points and diamond crossover at the junction in Poulton between the Blackpool North main line and the branch to Burn Naze. Campaigners for the reopening of the mothballed freight-only line breathed a deep sigh of relief as replacement of the junction with plain track would have effectively ruled out any hope of reinstating the link to Fleetwood.

Then, a year later in early 2008 NR renewed most of the remaining stretches of jointed track at locations including Devonshire Road bridge to Layton Station, Poulton, around the site of the former Weeton signal box, Kirkham and Salwick. Old wooden sleepers were replaced by the steel and concrete varieties, and old ballast was scraped away and new material laid.

The South Fylde branch had already been completely renewed by Railtrack with CWR and steel sleepers in 1997.

The following pictures by Paul Nettleton show the various stages of the Blackpool North line renewal.

An EWS Class 60 with a ballast train fails to distract the attention
of young footballers at Poulton-le-Fylde on 4 March 2007.

Above Class 66 No 66194 hauls a train of old track panels at Poulton Junction on 16 January 2005.

Below Poulton Junction is a hive of activity during a Network Rail project to renew the points leading to the mothballed Thornton line in a Sunday possession on 4 February 2007. A train of hoppers with No 66190 at the head tips ballast on to the up line from Blackpool North. The line to Thornton trails off to the right by Poulton No 3 signal box, soon becoming single track.

THE RAILWAYS OF BLACKPOOL AND THE FYLDE

Above Class 60 No 60045 and Class 66 No 66111 on infrastructure trains alongside a road-rail machine during engineering work at Poulton-le-Fylde on 11 March 2007.

Below With a long ballast train, EWS No 66213 powers through Poulton between the handsome station canopy and semaphore signals during track renewal work up the line at Kirkham in January 2008.

With the station building on the bridge in the background, Class 66 No 66135 is in the midst of engineering work just to the west of Kirkham & Wesham in February 2008.

Above EWS Class 66 No 66188 stands in the platform at Kirkham & Wesham Station with a ballast train during a track possession on Sunday 10 February 2008. Another, unidentified '66' is in the distance.

Below Under the glare of arc lights, Network Rail teams renew track during a night-time possession at Layton Station on 23 February 2008. The down line from near Plymouth Road bridge to Devonshire Road bridge was being renewed with continuously welded rail. Class 66 No 66197 stands with an infrastructure train, and two Class 60s were also involved in the operation, Nos 60017 and 60029 *Clitheroe Castle*. The 'switched-out' Blackpool North No 1 signal box was opened specially for the engineering work.

9.
MIGHT IN MINIATURE

Above The Pleasure Beach Express is a marvel in miniature, snaking sinuously between the big-thrill rides of Europe's largest amusement park. Hanging baskets decorate the grand LMS-style platform awning of the magnificent main station at the Pleasure Beach, with one-third-scale diesel-powered 'A3' 4-6-2 No 4472 *Mary Louise* standing at the head of a packed train on 30 July 1973. *Ray Ruffell, Silver Link Publishing collection*

Left The Pleasure Beach miniature railway is unusual in having its own fleet of replica, working, 21-inch-gauge goods wagons, some of which stand in the yard next to the main station and depot on 26 August 1971. They are not normally seen in use but add an air of authenticity to the scene. They include tank wagons, bogie flat wagons, four-wheeled box vans and tipping wagons. *Ray Ruffell, Silver Link Publishing collection*

This view, also from 26 August 1971, shows (from left) the monorail, the signal box, Hudswell Clarke 'Princess' 4-6-2 No 6200 *The Princess Royal*, dating from 1935, the goods yard with the engine shed and workshop behind, the water tower and the footbridge outside the station. *Ray Ruffell, Silver Link Publishing collection*

Above A rare glimpse inside the workshops of the Pleasure Beach Express on 26 August 1971. *Ray Ruffell, Silver Link Publishing collection*

Below The Pleasure Beach's miniature railway is celebrated for its attention to detail. The replica of the Forth Bridge that used to carry the line along the edge of the former boating lake has long disappeared but this delightful suspension bridge used to carry an even smaller miniature railway over the 'main line'. The miniature US-style 'streamliner' train, with members of the photographer's family waving to the camera, crosses the bridge on 30 July 1973. *Ray Ruffell, Silver Link Publishing collection*

Above Blackpool Pleasure Beach's other railway – the monorail that circumnavigates the amusement park – passes above the miniature railway yard and signal box on 30 July 1973. Opened in 1966 and running along a 1-mile route 35 feet above the ground, it was Britain's first commercial monorail. The vehicle bodies were built in Preston but the equipment was imported from Switzerland. *Ray Ruffell, Silver Link Publishing collection*

Right Wedged on to an extremely tight 42-acre site, the layout of the Pleasure Beach rides has to be meticulously planned and co-ordinated. Seen here on 26 August 1971, the miniature railway runs between the Turnpike car ride and the monorail. *Ray Ruffell, Silver Link Publishing collection*

Top This improbably bucolic Blackpool scene is less than 2 miles from the glitz of the Golden Mile. On 31 July 1973 Western-style steam-outline Rio Grande locomotive No 279 (Works No 7219) runs through the rustic scenery on the 15-inch-gauge Blackpool Zoo miniature railway. The 800-yard end-to-end line skirts the edge of the zoo, with the main station near the entrance to the attraction. *Ray Ruffell, Silver Link Publishing collection*

Middle Severn-Lamb Rio Grande 2-8-0 No 278 (Works No 7218) runs on the line at Blackpool Zoo on 25 October 1972, the year after the award-winning zoo opened on a former airfield site near Stanley Park. The two locomotives had 12-inch driving wheels and were powered by Ford 1,600cc petrol engines. In 1975 No 278 and five coaches were sold to the ill-fated line at Fleetwood (see Volume 1). *Ray Ruffell, Silver Link Publishing collection*

Bottom A 10¼-inch-gauge miniature railway used to operate at Jubilee Gardens near the seafront at Cleveleys in the 1970s and 1980s. On 21 July 1974 a train of happy passengers is hauled by a distinctively 'freelance'-design diesel locomotive! The wheel arrangement is believed to be 4-8-4. To the south of Blackpool, St Annes also has a miniature railway, a 15-inch-gauge rectangular loop around the seafront pitch-and-putt course near the resort's Pleasure Island complex. With a tunnel/stock shed at the back of the circuit, it is operated by a 15-inch-gauge Severn-Lamb locomotive, *St Annes Express*, dating from 1973. *Ray Ruffell, Silver Link Publishing collection*

10.
PRESTON AND THE WEST COAST MAIN LINE

Britain's busiest and most important mixed-traffic railway, the West Coast Main Line, is the principal inter-city artery to Preston, beyond which it feeds into Fylde services. As a result, the Fylde's railway fortunes – and therefore those of its tourism industry – are heavily dependent on the WCML.

The 400-mile former LNWR 'Premier Line', linking London with Manchester/Liverpool and Glasgow via the West Midlands, has been the subject of a series of ill-fated modernisation schemes. Plans to transform the infrastructure of the line, unveiled by Railtrack in 1997, had to be relaunched in 2002 after the original scheme went seriously over-budget and helped bring about the collapse of the national track-owning company. Originally due to cost £2.1 billion and scheduled for completion in 2005, the budget had spiralled to about £13 billion by the time Railtrack went into administration in October 2001.

Railtrack's successor, Network Rail, took over the project, which, in early 2008, was on course for completion in 2009 at an estimated cost of around £8 billion. This was partly achieved by the now-defunct Strategic Rail Authority having jettisoned Network Rail's plan to use so-called moving block signalling, which was untried and untested in the UK. A result of

this, however, was that Sir Richard Branson's Virgin Trains was forced to drop plans for 140mph running by its new £594 million 'Pendolino' tilting trains. But Virgin was able to launch a 125mph 'Pendolino' service from London to Manchester and Birmingham in the winter of 2004, leading to a 14 per cent annual increase in passenger numbers on the West Coast route and major cuts in journey times.

The problem for Blackpool and its sister resorts is that, while passengers are whisked to Preston in ultra-modern 'Pendolinos', they have to change there to sometimes overcrowded two-car 'Sprinter' units.

It's a world away from the heyday of the resort's rail services in the 1930s when the 'Blackpool and Fylde Coast Express' left Euston at 5.10pm every weekday except Saturday and arrived at Blackpool Central at 9.53pm. In the reverse direction it left Central at 8.25am, reaching Euston at 12.50pm. The final stage of the journey of 158 miles from Crewe to Euston was run in 154 minutes at an average start-to-stop speed of 61.6mph.

Today the 'Pendolinos' can travel at twice that speed but the days of the 'Blackpool and Fylde Coast Express' have passed, though whether the absence of a through link will be permanent remains to be seen.

Above Gateway to Blackpool: all traffic to and from the Fylde has to pass through the pivotal station at Preston. In Platform 6 on Friday 31 August 1962, young enthusiasts admire 'Duchess' 4-6-2 No 46223 *Princess Alice* at the head of the 9.30am Glasgow Central-Liverpool Exchange train. Preston's first station was opened by the North Union Railway in 1838. The present station was the result of a £250,000 reconstruction between 1877 and 1880, with the main entrance on Fishergate leading to a giant island platform 1,225 feet long and 100 feet wide beneath a new roof. The East Lancashire lines east of the main station were effectively a self-contained operation with their own station master and entrance; they closed on 1 May 1972. The station was given a major refit in the late 1990s costing more than £3 million, including refurbishment of Platforms 1 and 2 serving the Fylde Coast. Plans for further £20 million modernisation were announced in 2008. Until the introduction of restaurant cars in the 1890s, the main LNWR expresses made a 25-minute stop for passengers to dine. In both World Wars the station buffet became famous for serving free tea and snacks 24 hours a day to millions of service people, a volunteer operation that is commemorated by three plaques in the main waiting room on Platforms 3/4. *Ron Herbert*

Left The Preston & Wyre Railway originally ran from a two-platform station at Maudlands near the

Lancaster Canal basin in Preston, crossing the Lancaster & Preston Junction Railway on the level. The imposing ten-arch brick viaduct at Maudland remains one of the few major engineering structures on the otherwise flat line to the Fylde Coast. In 1846 the Fleetwood, Preston & West Riding Junction Railway also sought to use Maudlands as the terminus for a new line to Yorkshire, but the project failed to flourish. Initially the FPWRJ also crossed the LPJR route on the level, but the flat crossings were removed in June 1885 and the original Maudlands Bridge Station closed. In 1991, however, there was a flashback to the old P&W terminus when a temporary station was opened at Maudlands for one weekend only while work took place at the main station. It must have been one of the shortest-lived stations in railway history. Paul Nettleton, Chairman of Blackpool & Fylde Rail Users' Association, cuts the ribbon to open the temporary terminus, with Blackpool North Station Manager Barry Cole on the right. To the north-west of the temporary station site, part of the trackbed of the former quadruple-track section into Preston is now occupied by a stretch of the Tom Benson Way link road.

Top right The former LNWR engine shed at Preston is seen here in its heyday, with the automatic coaling plant to the left and the slender spire of St Walburge's Roman Catholic Church in the distance. The church was designed by architect Joseph Aloysius Hansom and built between 1850 and 1854. Locomotives visible include a 'Black Five' 4-6-0, ex-LNWR 0-8-0 goods engines and a Hughes-Fowler 'Crab' 2-6-0. The shed and turntable were on the west side of the main line, north of the station, and were developed by the LNWR. However, the depot was closed in 1961 after a fire, leaving the former L&Y Lostock Hall MPD as the only Preston shed. Lostock Hall was one of BR's last three steam sheds in the summer of 1968. *C. A. Appleton/J. A. Peden collection*

Above right A Brush Type 4 (later Class 47) diesel-electric locomotive hauls a tanker train off the branch from Preston Docks on to the West Coast Main Line, south of the station, in July 1974. The dock branch descended on a curved 1-in-29 gradient from the main line, then ran through a tunnel and across Strand Road. It was built in 1846 to ship coal from Victoria Quay to Wigan, but Preston Corporation acquired it and opened the Albert Edward Dock on 25 June 1892, after borrowing more than £650,000. Surrounded by

28 miles of railway, it was at the time the largest single dock in Britain, at 40 acres. In steam days trains from the dock were often banked up the incline by veteran LNWR 0-8-0s. It closed to commercial shipping in 1981 but the line is still in use for tanker trains to the bitumen works on the docks; these are hauled to the works from a new barrier-controlled crossing at Strand Road by locomotives from the preserved Ribble Steam Railway, which seamlessly blends heritage passenger and modern freight operations on its 1½-mile line. Formerly Steamport Southport, the RSR has one of the finest collections of industrial locomotives, both steam and diesel, in the UK, including some that formerly worked in the Fylde. The RSR has built a station, engine shed, museum and workshop – and runs over a working swingbridge, across the marina entrance. This means its timetable is dictated by the tide – the only preserved railway to have such a feature.

Across the Ribble, at Hesketh Bank between Preston and Southport, lies the narrow-gauge West Lancashire Light Railway, built by enthusiasts in 1967 and serving as a working museum for a variety of historic industrial locomotives from Britain and overseas. *Jack Fenton*

A former LNWR 4-6-0 approaches Preston Station from the north, with Dock Street Coal Sidings on the right, some time after the 1923 Grouping. The four-cylinder 4-6-0s of the 'Claughton' Class, named after No 2222 *Sir Gilbert Claughton*, were designed by C. J. Bowen-Cooke from 1913, and a total of 130 of the powerful locomotives were built. At its peak, Preston Station handled some 500 train days a day and even now deals with more than 250 services every weekday. *Edwin Ashworth/Ron Herbert collection*

The imposing former Park Hotel on East Cliff, seen in 1912, still dominates the southern approaches to Preston Station. Jointly owned by the LNWR and L&Y, it had a direct link to the platforms via a covered walkway and footbridge, and was advertised in timetables as being 'convenient for passengers to and from Scotland wishing to break their journey and also for visitors to the Lake District, Blackpool, Southport etc'. It is now local authority offices. *Commercial postcard*

This is the former North Union Railway bridge over the River Ribble in April 1972. Two signal arms are crossed out during the transitional period to colour lights from semaphore signalling in connection with the electrification of the northern section of the West Coast Main Line. The original North Union Railway viaduct, with five 120-foot arches, still carries the fast lines across the Ribble; it was widened in 1880 to carry the slow lines. *Jack Fenton*

South of Preston, the West Coast Main Line is quadruple-tracked. Near the multi-arched road bridge at Bee Lane, at Farington Curve Junction, BR 'Britannia' 4-6-2 No 70030 – leaking steam, minus its *William Wordsworth* nameplates, and with its reporting number 3X37 chalked on its smokebox door – makes a sad sight as it heads south in the mid-1960s. *Jack Fenton*

Above A Lancashire & Yorkshire Railway Aspinall 'Atlantic' heads a holiday train to Blackpool in 1912. It is probably on the four-track section of line south of Preston, owned by the LNWR as part of its 'Premier Line' between London and Scotland. Beyond Preston, however, the L&Y and LNWR ran the lines to Blackpool and Fleetwood jointly until their amalgamation on 1 January 1922, a year before becoming part of the LMS in the Grouping that created the 'Big Four' railway companies. *Commercial postcard*

Above right Barton & Broughton Station, north of Preston, dates back to 25 June 1840 and the opening of the Lancaster & Preston Junction Railway. The station was originally at Crow Hall but was moved north to School Lane in November 1840. It became Barton & Broughton in 1861, and closed on May Day 1939. It had a mix of brick and timber LNWR structures and a stone LPJR station building, some of which survive. A three-arch viaduct carries the line across Barton Brook. In this pre-war view, the station stands at the foot of the road bridge, with the signal box in the distance. *John Ryan collection*

Right Traversing a picturesque path between the Fylde plain to the west and the fells of the Forest of Bowland to the east, the Lancaster & Preston Junction Railway was opened on 25 June 1840, the public service beginning the next day. It was a competitor to the Lancaster Canal between Kendal and Preston, which had opened in 1797 with the barges taking more than 7 hours to cover the 57 miles. Despite this, within two years the LPJR's finances had become so parlous that its directors were forced to enter into an unprecedented agreement with the canal company, which from September 1842 leased the railway at a rent of £13,300 a year.

Beyond the north-eastern fringe of the Fylde, Galgate was one of the most dramatically located stations on the route, now part of the West Coast Main Line. Like Broughton, the station, the first stop south of Lancaster, was opened in June 1840 and, because of its elevated position, had no sidings. A six-arch viaduct 30 feet above the road and over the River Conder was a major engineering achievement. The first stone had been laid on Queen Victoria's Coronation day, 28 June 1838, and several Victoria Medals were deposited beneath it. The signal box had closed by 1905 and the station was shut by the LMS on 1 May 1939. The buildings were demolished before electrification of the line in the 1970s. *John Ryan collection*

Just north of the Fylde, the little port of Glasson Dock has enjoyed an improbably profitable and eventful history for its size. One of the oldest docks on the West Coast, it was opened in the late 18th century as a 'satellite' port for Lancaster, which was being restricted by the build-up of silt in the River Lune. In 1826 Glasson, near the Lune estuary, was linked by a 3-mile branch canal to the Lancaster Canal, giving it access to the prosperous towns of Preston to the south and Kendal to the north.

It was not until April 1883 that the railway arrived when the LNWR opened a 5½-mile branch line to a bay platform at the north end of Lancaster Castle Station. The passenger service started on 9 July. The line, with an intermediate station at Conder Green, served the Lune Mills of the linoleum manufacturer and local benefactor James Williamson, which had its own narrow-gauge railway system, worked by two Dick, Kerr 0-4-0Ts. Williamson, whose son later became Lord Ashton, also had his own private station at Ashton Hall. In contrast to the luxuries of the 'big house', the railwaymen's cottages nearby were without running water, electricity or gas. Freight traffic briefly flourished before the opening of Heysham Harbour in 1904, with Spanish ore being imported for Carnforth ironworks.

Although the Royal Train carrying King George V and Queen Mary was stabled overnight at Glasson Dock in 1917, passenger services were never a mainstay of the branch. From the 1920s two LNWR steam railcars worked services from a depot in Lancaster Bridge Road, but after many loss-making years the LMS finally shut its stations in July 1930.

Freight continued to be carried, however, and there was a daily goods trains over the full length of the branch until the 1940s. The line survived several closure attempts, helped largely by the continued traffic to and from Williamson's, but in July 1964 it was truncated at Lune Mills, then closed completely five years later. Although few signs of the railway remain, the port itself is still flourishing, particularly for leisure use, and it enjoyed a brief moment of notoriety during the 1984/85 miners' strike when it was used to import coal after pickets blockaded its larger North West neighbours.

Lancashire County Council has turned part of the former trackbed over the southern stretch of the line into a public footpath. In this picture from 1958, a solitary goods wagon stands abjectly in an overgrown siding near the buffer stops at Glasson Dock with the goods shed in the distance. *J. A. Peden*

11.
TRAMWAY
TRANSFORMATION

An £85.3 million tramway transformation will see 16 new lightweight, low-floor trams operating on Blackpool's famous seafront system by 2012. It will be accompanied by major infrastructure improvements, new tram stops and a showpiece depot at the tramway's Rigby Road headquarters. Somewhat poignantly, the depot for the new trams could be constructed on the council-owned car park in Blundell Street – the site of the resort's original tram shed. The late-Victorian shed, with its imposing façade and plaque proudly proclaiming 'Corporation Tramways', was demolished in 1982 but the site is earmarked as the hub of the proposed new network. The hope is that the new infrastructure will stand up better to the corrosive cocktail of wind-blown sea spray, salt and sand against which the tram system does daily battle.

For several years, as piecemeal modernisation has taken place, the network has been an incongruous combination of 'classic' tramway and modern light railway route. In 2005, for instance, the junction where trams turn off the seafront for the Hopton Road depot was renewed at a cost of nearly £1 million, funded by Whitehall. Yet it was 70-year-old vehicles that daily trundled over the hi-tech pointwork.

In February 2008 Rail Minister Tom Harris announced that the Government was contributing £60.3 million to the scheme to renew the entire 11½-mile length of the tramway between Fleetwood and Starr Gate, with work scheduled to start by the end of 2009. Blackpool Council and Lancashire County Council were each stumping up £12.5 million for the project, and the new trams should be running for the 2012 summer season.

Meanwhile, for the first time since it opened in 1885, the tramway was closed for its full length in the winter of 2007/08 for an 'emergency' £11.8 million infrastructure upgrade by contractors Birse and Colas Rail, including a new substation at Copse Road, Fleetwood, and renewing Pleasure Beach and Little Bispham loops. The section between Starr Gate and Uncle Tom's Cabin reopened on time for the Easter weekend, 21-24 March 2008, though completion of the work to the north was delayed until after the Bank Holiday and had a phased opening over the following weeks.

Before the work began, Blackpool Transport Services' Managing Director Steve Burd said that the summer of 2008 would see the resort's trams running on the best infrastructure they had had for years after the £11.8 million revitalisation. Some of the gated pedestrian crossing points on the segregated sleeper section of track between the Cabin and the Little Bispham loop have been taken out of commission to allow faster running speeds.

The emergency work left about 5 miles of the line remaining to be reconstructed as part of the 'supertram' scheme. This is a combination of paved track with embedded rail (on the Central and North Shore Promenades), conventional ballasted track sections between Cabin and Fleetwood (Fisherman's Walk) and the major section of street running from there to Fleetwood Ferry.

The latest upgrade will bring the network up to 21st-century standards and boost regeneration of the area. The investment is the centrepiece of the Government's response to the Blackpool Task Force report, which recommended ways to regenerate the area. The minister said:

'At over 120 years old, the Blackpool & Fleetwood Tramway is part of the local heritage as well as an important part of the local transport system. I want to make sure that tourists and local people alike can continue to enjoy the tramway in years to come and make sure it lies at the heart of the town's current regeneration plans.

We will continue to work with Blackpool Council, Lancashire County Council and local MPs so they can deliver a modern tramway that is attractive to passengers and value for money for the taxpayer. I am glad that we are working towards safeguarding the future of this iconic system for future generations.'

Tramway bosses had warned that, without more cash, the ageing system might even have to be shut down permanently. Already they have been forced to controversially mothball more than a third of the fleet, to keep a lid on costs as usage declines.

The bid to transform the historic seafront network into a modern public transport system has been on the table in various forms for several years. The fleet of modern trams would run alongside some of the refurbished classic vehicles that have formed the backbone of the tramway's services for three-quarters of a century. The new trams could cover the full line from Starr Gate to Fleetwood in 52 minutes. Overall, end-to-end journey times should improve by 15 minutes, owing to faster boarding and better acceleration of new vehicles, assisted by rationalising the stops.

The renovated heritage trams will be retained in service within the resort area for 30 years and for use on excursion journeys – for example, to manage demand during the Illuminations. The winter frequency of tram services will be doubled to every 10 minutes end-to-end – to be operated by the modern vehicles – interspersed with 10-minute Pleasure Beach to Cleveleys services at weekends and summer tourist periods, giving a 5-minute service within the resort area.

Tram passenger facilities will be fully upgraded, with dedicated platforms to assist boarding, and will provide, for example, shelters, seating, help points, information and litter bins. Government regulations will mean that all rail vehicles in scheduled passenger-carrying service must be fully accessible to disabled people by 2020.

However, it seems that plans for a Fylde-wide light rail system, with the tramway linking to the heavy rail line in South Shore and a new street tramway spur to North Station, have receded into the far distance. In 2003 proposals for a link from South Station along the former rail route to the town centre – now known as the Central Corridor – were scrapped apparently because the Government would not countenance the idea of duplicating the parallel tram route along the promenade.

In March 2008, however, the resort's regeneration company, ReBlackpool, announced it was looking into proposals for hybrid 'tram-trains' that would run on electricity on the tramway, then switch to diesel at a connection with Network Rail's South Fylde line at Burlington Road. ReBlackpool was applying for EU funding to investigate the possibility of introducing the tram service between Fleetwood/Blackpool and Preston. Soon afterwards, the Government announced a two-year trial with tram-trains on the Penistone Line between Barnsley and Huddersfield from 2010, though these would not be the 'hybrid' variety.

BAFRUA, however, was dismissive of the idea for the Fylde. Chairman Paul Nettleton wrote in the April/May 2008 edition of the association's journal, *Branch Line*:

'The main thing that ReBlackpool hasn't grasped is that it will be very difficult to integrate rolling stock with different maximum speeds if the hybrid tram could ever make it to Kirkham Junction.

The line speed on most of the Blackpool

North route is currently 70mph with a possibility that Network Rail could increase it to 90mph. There isn't a tram on this earth that could consistently run at high speeds in the same way as, say, a Class 185 TransPennine unit, which is actually rated at 100mph.'

He claimed the proposals would cause delays at Kirkham, and would distract attention from the real benefits that the Community Rail Partnership could bring in improving services on the route. 'I personally feel that all this is just a smokescreen to get rid of the line between Blackpool South and the Pleasure Beach and turn it into a car park.'

Even ReBlackpool admitted that there were a lot of obstacles to be overcome before the 'hybrid' trams could operate.

The tramway story

Blackpool's tramway opened on 29 September 1885 as a line of about 1¾ miles. Initially using the conduit system taking power from a groove between the tracks, it was a response by far-sighted Blackpool Corporation to the logistical problems of moving millions of visitors.

In 1898 the Blackpool & Fleetwood Tramroad Co opened a line along the clifftops between the two towns, taken over by Blackpool Corporation Tramways on New Year's Eve 1919. In Blackpool the tramway was extended along a series of 'inland' suburban routes, reaching its fullest extent in 1926.

In the 1930s General Manager Walter Luff introduced a fleet of Art Deco-influenced streamlined vehicles, many of which are still in operation today. In 1935 the trams carried almost 50 million visitors. There were also some less successful innovations, however, such as the handsome but problem-prone 'Coronation' cars of the 1950s.

Road competition ensured that by 1963 all the 'inland' routes had been replaced by buses. But Blackpool's genius as a tramway operator has always been its ability to reinvent itself, introducing continental-style twin cars in the 1960s then converting 1930s vehicles for one-person operation in the 1970s. In the 1980s Blackpool ordered the first totally new trams for 30 years, the 'Centenary' cars. But despite the ingenuity of managers and workers at the depot off Rigby Road, the strains were starting to show.

At least a dozen trams are visible in this spectacular aerial view of a crowded Blackpool seafront between North and Central Piers in the late 1930s. The tide is going out as bathers and boats throng the beach and foreshore. To the right is the vast expanse of Central Station. *Commercial postcard*

The Blackpool & Fleetwood Tramway today carries nearly four million passengers a year, around 75 per cent of whom are visitors to Blackpool. Traffic is highly seasonal. Weekly farebox income varies from £9,000 in winter to around £250,000 during the Illuminations, but the tramway provides only about 6 per cent of the total profit of the BTS, which is wholly owned by Blackpool Council but operated at 'arm's length'. The council owns the track, overhead and the buildings on the Rigby Road site used for storage and maintenance of trams, while the trams and buses themselves and the rest of the site are owned by the BTS. Blackpool Council's Streetscene Division maintains the tracks, while electrical maintenance is subcontracted to BTS, both at the expense of the borough and county councils.

The developments are being closely monitored by preservation organisation Lancastrian Transport Trust and by the influential 600-strong Fylde Tramway Society, formed in 1971, and with members from all over the world. Every year the Trust hosts one of the North West's biggest transport festivals, 'Totally Transport', a gathering of hundreds of classic and modern trams, buses, cars, coaches and commercial vehicles on the promenade. With more than 40 trams and buses in its ownership, LTT has been in talks with council officials in a bid to secure a permanent venue for its long-term vision of a year-round, themed transport attraction.

Websites

Lancastrian Transport Trust:
   www.ltt.org.uk
Fylde Tramway Society:
   www.fyldetramwaysociety.co.uk
Blackpool Transport Services Ltd:
   www.blackpooltransport.com

Open-top Lytham St Annes tram No 2 is en route towards Blackpool along Clifton Drive North through the desolate sand dunes between the two resorts around 1916. Three passengers pose formally for the camera. The tramway had opened in 1896 and until 1903 the trams were gas-powered. The drifting sand clogging the rails was one of the factors that led to the closure of the St Annes-Lytham section in December 1936 and the complete abandonment of the system the following April.

One of the streamlined single-deck railcoaches, introduced by renowned Transport Department General Manager Walter Luff in the 1930s, heads from Talbot Square past the War Memorial on Princess Parade in 1964. Apart from the lines to the depot, the stretch of track past the Metropole Hotel was by then the only section of street-running tramway left in Blackpool. *Commercial postcard*

Above Two of the huge 'Dreadnought' trams stand outside the entrance to North Pier around 1904. Built between 1898 and 1903, the 'Dreadnoughts' could seat 86 and their twin staircases, front and back, made for fast loading. *Commercial postcard*

Right The Circular Tour from Talbot Square through Marton was one of the most popular trips on the tramway in the early years of the 20th century. Packed 'Toastrack' car No 78 heads along Whitegate Drive on the easternmost leg of the journey. Twenty-four of the 69-seat cars were built by UEC in Preston between 1911 and 1914 and survived until the early 1940s. *Commercial postcard*

Right Blackpool's illuminated trams were the stars of the autumn 'Lights'. One of the most colourful was the brightly lit 'Progress' car, bearing the legend 'Welcome to our visitors via land, sea or air', though the display could be altered. For instance, for the Queen's Coronation in 1953 it proclaimed 'Long may she reign'. The tram was built at a cost of £2,500 for the first post-war Illuminations in 1949, based on the old wartime 'Bandwagon' vehicle. The corporation's body-shop gave it the appearance of a 'Balloon' double-decker, with 'shadow' passengers in the windows. *Commercial postcard*

TRAMWAY TRANSFORMATION

Above Enclosed and open-balcony Standard trams and an open single-decker tour bus are seen in Talbot Square, alongside Sacred Heart Roman Catholic Church, Yates's Wine Lodge and (right) the Town Hall in the 1930s. The line ran up Talbot Road to Layton until October 1936, when the trams were replaced by Walter Luff's streamlined Leyland Titan buses. *Commercial postcard*

Below On a damp day in the 1960s, Standard tram No 160 heads south past Waterloo Road towards Starr Gate near the Dutton Arms pub on South Promenade. Beyond the Ford Anglia to the left is the former Lion pub, now Yates's Wine Lodge. *Judd Bros/Jack Fenton collection*

Above The Blackpool tramway celebrated its centenary in 1985 with a series of spectacular parades and other special events. On 7 September, visiting Manchester car No 765 (foreground), restored 1928 Blackpool & Fleetwood 'Pantograph' tram No 167 and Blackpool 'Balloon' No 715 stand at Fleetwood Ferry – the visitor was working a Manchester Locomotive Club special! *Ray Ruffell, Silver Link Publishing collection*

Right Blackpool's 'Dreadnought' trams were as imposing as the supposedly impregnable battleships after which they were named (the trams were built shortly before the L&Y 4-6-0s of the same name). Car No 59, built in 1902, is the only survivor of the fleet and was recovered from an undignified retirement at the back of a tram shed in 1959; it was painstakingly restored for the 75th anniversary of the tramway the following year. In 1985 it was one of the stars of the centenary celebrations when it returned from the National Tramway Museum at Crich for the anniversary procession. With top-deck passengers well wrapped up against the elements, it is seen coasting along Lord Street in Fleetwood as part of the seventh annual convention weekend of the Fylde Tramway Society in 1985. *The Gazette*

Above On a glorious summer's day, 'Vanguard' car No 619 stands on the clifftop section, en route to Manchester Square, while passengers leave Bispham-bound 'Balloon' double-decker No 704, one of the classic streamliners dating from the 1930s. The replica crossbench car was built to mark the centenary of the Blackpool & Fleetwood Tramroad in 1998. *Glynn Hague*

Below Threatening skies loom above southbound English Electric 'Balloon' double-decker No 262 on the clifftop sleeper-track section of the tramway on Sunday 18 April 1965 – possibly Easter Day. The sleek, streamlined 'Balloons', with 94 seats, were introduced as part of Walter Luff's modernisation of the fleet in the 1930s. *Ron Herbert*

Above A spring shower has left the tracks glistening as single-deck English Electric railcoach No 265 stands at North Pier on Monday 19 April 1965, with a blue Leyland Lytham St Annes double-decker bus in the background on the No 11 route to St Annes. *Ron Herbert*

Below Twin-car set Nos 276/271 heads towards the Pleasure Beach on 29 August 1964, followed by a 'Balloon' double-decker. The twin cars were developed from 1958, converted from 1930s railcoaches. The distinctive 'Polo'-shaped signs like the one on the waiting shelter were typical of the resort's tramway at this time. *Ron Herbert*

Above Railcoaches heading north to Cleveleys (left) and south to the Pleasure Beach pass on the Golden Mile, with its stalls advertising 'Jugs of tea for the sands', in a bustling scene from the 1960s.

Below This is a scene that had vanished from virtually every other conurbation in Britain when this picture was taken: a tram rattling past shops and terraced houses in a town centre. Only this, of course, is not an inland industrial town but Fleetwood, and 'Balloon' car No 247 has just branched off the double-track section and is about to take the curve into Bold Street on the loop to the terminus at Fleetwood Ferry. The original 1899 tram depot, demolished in 1973, is in the background and the port's hospital on the left.

Above A group of enthusiasts prepares to embark on a tour of the tramway on board 'Dreadnought' No 59 at the Rigby Road depot in the 1960s, with illuminated Standard car No 158 on the left. In 1959 Nos 158 and 159 were embellished with rows of lamps with illuminated stars at each end, and the slogan 'Welcome to Blackpool Illuminations' on the sides.

Below Many decades earlier, Edwardian visitors throng Central Promenade as a 'Dreadnought' car makes its stately progress towards North Shore, with Central Pier in the background.

Left Time and intensive use have taken their toll on the segregated sleeper-track section of the tramway north of Cleveleys, seen during an inspection in 2007. Passengers experienced rough riding on parts of the tramway, with the vehicles yawing and visible distortions on the track. *Blackpool Borough Council*

Below In the winter of 2004/05, trams returned to the world's oldest section of electric street tramway, along Blundell Street and Princess Street. The reason for the diversion was a major project to renew the points and track at Manchester Square, where trams branch off the Promenade for the Rigby Road depot; this left the single-track 'Foxhall' line as the only route to the prom. On 27 February 2005 Standard No 147 receives attention to its trolley pole as it negotiates the tight curve from Blundell Street into Princess Street during the 'By Tram to Foxhall' event organised by the Lancastrian Transport Trust. *LTT*

Above Exquisitely turned out in 'wartime' green livery, 'Balloon' double-decker No 700 heads along Blundell Street towards the Promenade during the LTT's 'By Tram to Foxhall' event on 27 February 2005. To the right is the site of the former Blundell Street tram shed – earmarked as the location of the depot for the resort's planned fleet of 16 new low-floor trams. *LTT*

Right Blackpool MPs join the celebrations after the announcement that Blackpool's £85 million tramway revamp had been approved by the Government in February 2008. Standing on the left is Town Crier Barry McQueen. Sitting (left to right) are Joan Humble, MP for Blackpool North and Fleetwood, Jackie Potter, Executive Director for Regeneration and Tourism at Blackpool Council, Rail Minister Tom Harris and Gordon Marsden, MP for Blackpool South. Phil Wright, Managing Director of Birse Coastal (centre, rear), is flanked by two construction workers. *Blackpool Borough Council*

SUPPLEMENTARY BIBLIOGRAPHY

The following references are in addition to those listed in Volume 1.

Baker, S. K. *Rail Atlas of Britain and Ireland*, 4th ed (OPC, 1984)

Butterell, R., Holroyde, D. and Townsend, S. *abc Miniature Railways* (Ian Allan, 1998)

Christiansen, R. *Regional Rail Centres: North West* (Ian Allan, 1995)

Harris, M. 'Special Traffic – Blackpool' (*Steam Days*, August 2001)

Johnston, H. (ed) *The Comprehensive Guide to Britain's Railways*, 11th Edition (Bauer Active, 2008)

Nock, O. S. *The Pocket Encyclopaedia of British Steam Locomotives* (Blandford Press, 1973)

Palmer, S. *Blackpool & Fleetwood by Tram* (Platform 5, 1988)

Blackpool's Trams Past & Present (Venture Publications, 2007)

Ramsbottom, M. and Pickup, C. *The Preston to Wyre Railway* (Hedgehog Historical Publications, 1996)

Shannon, P. and Hillmer, J. *British Railways Past and Present No 43: West, East and North Lancashire* (Past & Present Publishing, 2004)

Suggitt, G. *Lost Railways of Lancashire* (Countryside Books, 2003)

INDEX